Rise Up

& Repeal

A Poetic Archive
of the 8th Amendment

Edited by Sarah Brazil
and Sarah Bernstein

Published by Sad Press

May 2019

978-1-912802-24-1

Set in Goudy Old Style, Garamond,
Dyslexie, and Bakery

Preface

This collection has only been possible through collaboration and generosity. All poems have been freely offered by contributors. The support and inspiration that co-editor Sarah Bernstein, and publishing team Samantha Walton and Jo Lindsay Walton, have offered throughout has been nothing short of remarkable. All three have been convinced of the importance of this work since I mumbled its possibility in a research institute in Edinburgh, and have given time and energy while asking nothing in return.

The project began, of all places, on social media, where I witnessed an abundance of poetry posted online throughout the Repeal the Eighth Amendment campaign. As a student and teacher of literature, I believe in its social and everyday importance—that stories are part of what it means to be human. These poems are proof that poetry is not elitist, but is by and for everyone. The poems compiled in this collection are from professional poets and people who do not consider themselves to be poets. In some instances, the poems were written as a spontaneous attempt to capture a feeling, to articulate something vital that ordinary language couldn't. In some instances, contributors offered things other than poems, and we happily welcomed them.

The poems in this collection capture the years of struggle that led to the Yes vote in the Irish referendum on the Eighth Amendment, a law that had made the life of a woman equivalent to a fertilised egg. They voice social disparities that have gone unspoken for centuries. They are of the utmost urgency, and put into poetic form the struggles of women, in Ireland and elsewhere, for basic dignity and fundamental human rights.

These struggles continue today in many forms. As this preface is being written, the Eighth Amendment has only just been removed from the Irish Constitution and there is no current provision for abortion or compassionate termination services in Ireland. Abortion remains illegal in Northern Ireland, which is constitutionally adrift from the rest of the UK on this issue. Rape continues to be a prolific crime that is underreported, with police services underfunded and insufficiently trained to support victims. Domestic violence is still a substantial risk to women. Women are underpaid for their contribution to the workplace and society at large. They are harassed at work and on the street. Childcare continues to be expensive, and little social support exists for parents. But there is hope. Discourses are being established to give women a language to speak to each other about their struggles, to report behaviour, and to find new channels of highlighting injustice. This collection is part of the increasing vocalisation of and fight for a fairer future.

Most of us involved have entered this project as novices of one sort or another. This collection is a departure from the editorial and publishing teams' daily work, and the contributors too have taken a leap of faith into the unknown. It is new ground in many senses. All have been convinced, however, of the value of what this collection can offer. It is an archive of a period in Irish and world history that is unlike anything we have seen before. But it is also an intervention into the current conversations of what literature can do for us. The poets give voice to resistance against the many forms of oppression they identify. The poems are rallying cries, they are experiences of anguish, hope, and love. They are political. They are calls to be compassionate, to care for our fellow citizens and their needs. To overcome the legacies of religious domination and abuse, and to move beyond patriarchal nationalism.

I want to thank each poet deeply for their trust in me, and to thank Sarah, Sam, and Jo for their faith in the project. It has been a privilege to be the compiler and co-editor of this collection. All proceeds from sales will be donated to the charities and organisations that continue to be the stalwarts of helping twelve women in Ireland access abortion services each day.

This collection is dedicated to the hundreds of thousands of people who have been affected by the Eigth Amendment. To Savita Halappanavar and her family—its most prominent and unwilling victim—to Ann Lovett, and to all others who suffer at the hands of cruel and regressive abortion laws, in Ireland and worldwide.

Ní saoirse go saoirse na mBan.

There is no freedom until the freedom of women.

Sarah Brazil
October 2018

Contents

What Stories Will Tell Us and Our Lives?

Thou – Lucia Sellars

The Birth of Rain – Udita Banerjee

Deconstruction – Frances Presley

One Sings, the Other Doesn't: A Reproductive Rights Musical for the Moment – So Mayer

A Statistically Average Day in 21st Century Ireland – Emer Ellis-Neenan

10 Telechirics in Anticipation of the Vote – Sarah Hayden

I Have a Friend – Maria Haughey

Mná: Is Gnáthóg Sibh (Women: You are Home)

Rann – Caitlín Doherty

Radical Doula – Sally-Shakti Willow

Uprising – Kate Went

RU 486 – So Mayer

From *Transpositions* – Sophie Seita & Jasmine Brady

Fade – Alice Tarbuck

ariel – Alice Tarbuck

We that Give It

Choice – Caoimhe Kenny

Rebel Girl Repeal – Erin Darcy

The Work and its Record – Holly Pester

8 – Aoife Hynes

The Wave – Sinéad O' Rourke

A Chapter Has Closed

Because of You – Dee Dickens
Elation – Steve Gannon
Repealed – Sarah Gallagher
Relief – Marianna Donnart
For Whom the Bells Toll Newly – Andre Archimbaud
#Repealedthe8th – Gráinne Gillis

Ireland is a
Catholic Country

Playing Chicken

The doctor reads the notes
on the back of what used to be
called a TV dinner.
How many minutes
if the wattage isn't clearly
marked on the machine?
She thinks of the woman
with a heartbeat in her belly,
her agonising moans, the wait
and see, the day
and night, the wondering
if this too shall pass.
Patient, temperature soaring
and still it goes on, the shake
of tired heads, the useless
whispers, the wringing
of tied hands.
The bell dings.
Another push on the
button ...
just to be sure.

~ Fi Smith

An Amendment

Daughters, Sisters, Mothers, Lovers.
These are the women of Ireland.
These are the women of Ireland and that is their greatest sin.

Because an amendment is written somewhere,
I am a vessel that once full has no voice,
No agency, No autonomy, No voice for my choice.
My life of highs and lows, of loves and laughs, of tears and pain,
is equated to something whose life has yet to begin.

Because an amendment is written somewhere,
a woman that yearns to be a mother will yearn all her whole life.
Sterilization before termination resulting in a lost generation.

Because an amendment is written somewhere,
we force a woman to bear and watch her child live a short, pain-filled life.
No compassion. No connection. Quantity, not quality.

Because an amendment is written somewhere,
tonight in Ireland, a woman lies in the foetal position:
in fear and in pain, knowing her life will never be the same.
Unregulated. Unsupported. Undocumented. Unknown.

Because an amendment is written somewhere,
tomorrow we export our problem abroad.
Twelve women a day we send on their way:
out of sight, out of mind. Silenced through shame.

Because an amendment is written somewhere,
a daughter grows up not knowing her mum.
That woman's crime: getting sick and being pregnant at the same time.
No greater equality in life than when mother and child
are buried side by side.

We are your daughters.
We are your sisters.
We are your mothers.
We are your lovers.
We are the women of Ireland.
We are the women of Ireland and that should no longer be our greatest sin.

~ Kate Mitchell

Dragon Egg

You ascend, taking up residence in
a fortress of clouds but lower than the Gods,
you are now a spectator.

The zip. The belt. The sounds you remember.
Missed calls from your mother,
she left the key under the flowerpot filled with dying geraniums.

And she's strict. You are not allowed read teen magazines,
you don't know any better, maybe it's normal,
and you're just being paranoid.

You can't remember how to get home, this road you take home
        from school every day.
The colour seeped out of the world.
But you remember the gravel.

You could kiss it, the gravel, just for being solid.
You try to sprout roots down into it,
but they are weak and stringy.

You believed what came later to be a dragon in your belly,
it would burn you from the inside out.
They would find your charred remains under the hay bales on which
        you once played.

You were too young. You googled methods.
Coat hangers, a fall from stairs, bathroom chemicals,
    gaping holes in your private school education, knowing nothing
    beyond white knee length socks and a kilt.

You blamed it on the school disco. Your mother's shame became
    your shackle.
The head sat at her throne, divided from her subjects by a desk.
Your mother made another call.

"Don't tell your father." You wouldn't anyway.
Your mother gets sea sick. But you don't. Your head bursting with
    his unspoken name.
And later, swinging your legs on a chair in a blue waiting room.
    They call your name.

And when you bled, you fantasised that the blood dribbling from
    between your legs would become the sea.

You, the mystic child, would walk across it.

~ Amy Dwyer

Subtext 1978

after Pascal O'Loughlin's Now Legwarmers

marion and angela are missing   as kate   flays her arms   girl amaryllis

marion and angela are missing   as stanerra   stumbles   infant horse kicks

marion and angela are missing   as swanzy   orphist darling   expires

marion and angela are missing   as dublin   sends its housing   to the stocks

marion and angela are missing   as clonduff estate is fiction non fiction

marion and angela are missing   as animals   roadkill   making the break

marion and angela are missing   as david ditched   diamond dogs   for berlin

marion and angela are missing   as deirdre   lost sisters   drumcondra

marion and angela are missing   as the gardai are looking not looking

marion and angela are missing   as she is a sisters of mercy song

marion and angela are missing   as they are   of charity   of refuge

marion and angela are missing   as they are   a catholic   dirty secret

marion and angela are missing   as they were   frightened women   lost children

marion and angela are missing   as she was   older sibling   goth princess

marion and angela are missing   as she was   the best friend   he ever had

marion and angela are missing   as they were   too damn poor   to fly solo

marion and angela are missing   as they were   too damn flash   for the disgrace

marion and angela were missing   but they are   too damn late   for repeal

~ Sarah Crewe

Possessing Nothing

In 1996 Nuala O'Faolain wrote that 'there are no typical people. And places don't stay the same. The world changed around Ireland, and even Ireland changed' (*Are You Somebody?* 1996, x). O'Faolain was, like myself, one of the *other* kinds of women. The ones who don't have children, who haven't married up and settled down, and whose presence in the public sphere causes shiftiness or embarrassment, depending on whether the company feels pity, or awkwardness, or just plain curiosity. Childlessness is presumed as a sad accident, a missed opportunity, or concealed tragedy: as I edge toward the impossibility of conception, I wonder if I am implictly divested of the right to comment on the meaning of maternity despite a lifetime of investment in feminism. O'Faolain's memoir tells a story which doesn't fit the narrative she expected from life: it possesses 'nothing that had traditionally mattered to women' (xi). O'Faolain's confessional was one of the first harbingers of Ireland's suppressed narratives, brought to full voice in the Ryan Report – that encyclopedia of violence and shame. O'Faolain's story engendered a public response: an avalanche of letters which told answering stories, 'telling out ... pain' (224) and sympathy. Stories *do* things to people. The referendum on the repeal of the eighth amendment was won by narrative. The telling of stories from individual women took on the power of narrative: the cumulative energy of all story-telling. For the lifetime of the state itself, men and women left it to those with English accents to form the word *abortion* as if the very word might pollute Irish mouths, attach itself to the windpipe and work down to the stomach. To speak these stories was activism and radical public vulnerability. Legal fictions had for so long made these narratives impossible: but narrative was necessary to make change happen. Online initiatives such as *In Her Shoes* used narrative to make those vacant bodies real and suffering. Publishing women's abortion stories – outlining the financial, emotional and personal suffering of women seeking terminations, these personal stories made abortion part of a longer narrative. These stories expanded the public sphere's capacity for distributing empathy amongst all citizens, a political prerequisite to allowing women fuller participation in civil life. This astonishing permutation allowed women to speak of their bodies and fertility in new and significant ways.

I teach fiction at the most Westerly university in Europe, in a seaboard city whose flood-prone streets lead out to a bay braced against the Atlantic by a shoulder of karst limestone. Galway thinks of itself as cosmopolitan: cultural, creative, a city of blow-ins, intellectuals and artists liberated by its distance from the centre of power. It's a myth, of course: as much as any other, it's a city of bourgeois Irish attitudes and backwater self-indulgence, of performative bohemianism masking crushing artistic inadequacy, a scaled-down dumbshow of urban living staged for tourists and culchies. Its population swells during university semesters. Students pour in from Western counties, the midlands, a handful from Dublin and Cork. Despite the bland perfection of its glossy promotional images, Galway shares all of modern Ireland's problems: surrounded by jerry-built estates hiked up during the boom years, served by a decrepit Hospital, and labouring under an acute housing crisis. Ireland, more than most nations, is built on a culture of wilful disregard. It labours to collectively ignore vast infrastuctures of exclusion, immiseration and injustice to allow its rickety state apparatus to continue. In a five year span, Ireland has seen scandals over Garda corruption; illegal falsification of adoption consent forms; outrage over mass mortality in Mother and Baby homes in Tuam; and the entirely avoidable death of a woman in a maternity ward in University Hospital Galway. This litany of state-sanctioned offences makes Repeal a small but significant victory, rather than a revolutionary turning point. It is, more accurately, another partial catharsis in the past two decades move to tell stories which have in truth been known for a longer time.

Yet stories bind you into the changing world, atypical or not. One of the novels I teach is Mike McCormack's 2016 novel *Solar Bones*. In it, the narrator's daughter Agnes is the kind of arty, intelligent, intense young woman I have often met in the West of Ireland. A meditation on the morality of Irish masculinity and politics, McCormack's novel explores the male presumption that the state shares a paternalist care for his daughter. The registration of her birth certificate becomes a quasi-sacramental celebration of her nascent political rights: the new father eulogizes 'the seal ... set on her identity as an Irish citizen ... the point of all the massive overarching state apparatus within which she could live out her life as a free and self-determining individual ... a political index which held a space for her in the state's mindfulness' (39).

In adulthood, however, Agnes' artistic expression undermines this faith: her first exhibtion in a Galway gallery is an installation piece created in which crime headlines culled from local newspapers are painted onto the walls in her own blood, harvested over weeks. His daughter's blood (it's unclear whether it includes, or indeed is entirely made up of, menstrual blood) provokes a kind of paternal panic attack in Marcus Conway. He sweats under a 'shamed helplessness' (54) that he has "failed [his] daughter ... had I pushed towards this ... the conviction hardening within me that having lived a decent life might not in itself be enough – or a life which till now I had honestly thought was decent ... [there is] some definite charge or accusation in the air' (54). That accusation – that Ireland's template for a 'decent life' does not take women's experience into account and has wounded and cost women dearly, resting, as it does, upon a constitution which renders women as mothers, vassals, wives – reverberates through the latter half of the novel. Marcus' assumption of the care-giving role to his wife Mairead suggests the need for empathetic models of masculinity, even as her sickness (the result of cryptospiridium poisoning in the water supply) further indicts the state's disregard for the rural population, and for women in particular. In Sally Rooney's *Conversations with Friends* (2017), the cataclysmic pain and bleeding caused by endometriosis is initially misread by the narrator as pregnancy symptoms: a somatic sign of her physical and legal vulnerability at the nexus of a complex set of relationships. But Frances' crippling bleeding is diagnosed not as a miscarriage, but endometriosis. What she initially reads – in the manner of the Irish narrative fatalism – as the classic problem of uncontrolled fertility is transmuted into a diagnosis which raises the possibility of infertility. Bleeding heavily, she muses that at least now she 'didn't need to consider things like Irish constitutional law, the right to travel, my current bank balance, and so on' (169).

Both these novels were written under the eighth amendment and both register, in non-sensational fashion, the quotidian discomfort and marginalisation of women. Rooney, as she plangently noted, 'was born twenty seven years ... before the repeal of the Eighth Amendment' (*London Review of Books*, Vol. 40 No. 10 · 24 May 2018, p. 16): thus living the majority of her reproductive life with little legal autonomy. What does that do to a sense of self? How does that mean for political citizenship? What is an aside in *Conversations with Friends* signals the foreclosure of possibility pregnancy would entail. McCormack teaches Creative Writing at the National University of Ireland, Galway: a few minutes walk from the hospital where Savita Halappanavar died from a heart-attack brought on by sepsis caused by a miscarriage. Halpannavar was told by midwives that an abortion was impossible despite the unviability of the fetus, and that she would have to wait until her life was sufficiently in danger to be relieved of the pregnancy. Reading such literature with women who walk by the Hospital on their way to seminars and whose own personhood has been constitutionally constrained for the entirety of their young lives gives each story of maternity and sexuality a rill of anxiety: how do we imagine bodies and selves here? What stories will tell us and our lives?

Politics requires narratives. Ireland's story is particularly insecure since its own political beginnings are no more than a failed birth: the man-midwives of the Free State ignoring the chewed umbilical of the border trailing across its midriff. Repeal risked repeating the construction of woman-as-mother even if only as woman-as-mother-to-be. It emphasized, by necessity, those stories of brutalisation and unnecessary suffering caused by legislation. It had to echo the moral norms of procreation and family life. Like marriage equality, it was a moment which was (in some ways) a renewal of social ties and which affirmed the centrality of maternity and pregnancy to women's experience. Political rhetoric demands language be more powerful than subtle or radical. In global contexts of antifeminist legislation and reproductive injustice, the repeal of the eighth amendment might look like progress. But in longer narratives of nation and history, such optimism looks less certain. Ireland's referendum exposes Britain's long legislative denial about the misogynist junta it bolsters in Northern Ireland and the blithe indifference of generations of English feminists to women's suffering in the same jurisdiction. Abortion rights cut straight to the heart of hypocrisy. Repeal frees us to shape old narratives in new ways, to tell stories which had been overlaid by euphemism, silence, indirection, Ireland's skilled legerdemain of shame. Even those who voted against are capable of a new moral agency because we can never know ourselves until our stories diverge from the plots we expect. But this moment of apparent democratic process is only part of a story about humanity's capacity for self-harm as well as for progress, its ability to change its mind when confronted by complex stories that demand empathy. Stories of progress are powerful and comforting, but they look like episodes of sense in humanity's absurdist sprawl. After all, the eighth amendment was only inserted after a referendum in 1983.

Repeal is thus Ireland's most recent crisis of *reproduction*, in the most fundamental fashion. But it is also a 'crisis of reproduction ... when the social formation can no longer be reproduced on the basis of the pre-existing system of social relations' (Stuart Hall and Bill Schwartz, *Crisis in the British State*, 1985, p. 9). Ireland's narrative institutions, the dysfunctional fictions which buried its secrets and its women in lyric pain, no longer suffices for anyone. It is the time to expunge toxic narratives, to replace and rejuvenate them so that this moment of crisis can also become 'a moment of reconstruction...' like O'Faolain's 'telling of pain' becoming 'the means by which social relations are reconstituted'. Those unlicensed stories are the means for Ireland to change, to harness the powers of individual narrative: each pregnancy becoming a matter of interpretive responsibility, rather than a plot device which sends us toward preordained futures. Paradoxically, abortion *generates* the possibility of other narratives, other futures – some of them 'possessing nothing which has traditionally mattered to women'. Repeal is not an end in itself but the possibility of a radical proliferation of narratives for women: ones which don't necessarily end in reproduction, shame for having children, or not having them. It opens up a space in which we might imagine multiple forms of being persons and citizens, equally valued and valuable, new narratives through which to remake the state of being itself.

~ Rebecca Anne Barr

Five Sorrowful Mysteries

Five sorrowful mysteries
embedded in our history
shadow every woman
fearing the apparition
of a cross
on the plastic screen
of a pregnancy test.
For, you see, Ireland is a Catholic country
and the rosary needs
its five sorrowful mysteries.

The first sorrowful mystery –
a teenage girl bleeding out
upon the feet of the perennial virgin
who eyes her with disdain.

The second and third sorrowful mysteries –
two women, decades apart
left to watch the clock run out
as cancer savages their bodies.
One, denied care and abandoned to die,
the other
dragged from the brink and driven from home
for a procedure

that should have been her saviour
to learn, on return,
the delay is terminal.
Two women deemed by state
too insignificant to save.

The fourth sorrowful mystery –
a young couple broken
by an approaching foetal fatality.
A woman's life hangs on a wire
but her plea for survival is refused
for the futile push to save the other.
Her husband makes the journey home, alone,
to a lingering silence.

The fifth sorrowful mystery –
a mother and father
unable to grieve their daughter
whose lifeless shell
is forced to remain to sustain
the ebbing life within her.

There is no mystery here.
This is because
"Ireland is a Catholic country,"
because near two millennia of biblical oppression
dictates

that woman was made
from the rib of man
to receive, conceive, gestate, and produce.

But today,
this is an Ireland that will not worship
at the grotto of your indifference.
On May 25th, Ireland spoke
in voices that could not be ignored.
You have failed our women in their hundreds
but you will fail no more.

~ Natasha Helen Crudden

Holy Has No Place Here

Isle of Empathy

Isle of invisible drunken tramps
Half of them ravaged by your saints and scholars
Then dumped from your ashtray of industrial schools
Trying to wash themselves clean with the bottle

Isle of stop letting foreigners in
With their workers' hands and their hungry mouths
Ready to take the food from our tables
Where there's no place for skin darker than ours

Isle of forcing motherhood
On girls too young to see over a pram
Because each child is cherished equally
Except the ones too poor for the boat

Isle of twitching curtains and gossiping tongues
Over pots of tea and Angelus bells
But silence in the witness box
If he heard it first in confession

Isle of not on my doorstep – junkies rob
But keep them on the methadone
Because zombies can't hop garden walls
When they barely know their own name

Isle of canonising the Irish mammy
Rewarding her with chains of gold
Handy for tying her to the kitchen sink
And making her thank you for it

Isle of young men swinging from shower rails
Because they've been told that boys don't cry
Go out and get a job or just have a pint
No son of mine will be a poof

Isle of babies in septic tanks
Next to siblings not quite a year older
But their mother had been in the laundry for five
Washing white collars for men with brass necks

Isle of report any unexplained wealth
Remember that dole cheats cheat us all
But offshore accounts don't count as cheating
If you're wearing a tie you're just savvy

Isle of "we all" lost the run of ourselves
So now pay the piper, it's ten grand a head
Get up off your arse unless it's to protest
Then you're nothing but a gurrier

Isle of sorry for your troubles but hang on till you bleed
We don't like to give abortion type drugs
It is what it is, you'll just have to wait
This is a Catholic country

Isle of children in B&Bs
Thousands are homeless, how sad
But talk to Joe about the rapid build
Going up next to your private estate

Isle of pensioners falling at home
And no one coming to help
Not enough hours from the HSE
Frozen for fear of turning on the heat

Isle of prison time for no TV licence
None for those who rob through the letterbox
It's hard to pull yourself up by your bootstraps
If you never had any boots

Isle of cervical and anti-d scandals
Isle of symphysiotomies
Isle that hates notions and delusions of grandeur
But sold our souls for respectability

Isle that said fuck the fabric of society
Love is love, yes equality
Isle that says we are better than this
Isle that says Together For Yes.

~ Doireann the Don O' Neill

In Our Hands

Don't tell me that I have blood on my hands
with your snow white assumption,
grasping your beads as if your heart pumps only with love,
and your veins run with blood that's blue like the cloak of the Virgin.

The only blue I can find is that of the lips of a girl,
as the chill of the night finds its way into her
in a way that she never expected.

Don't tell me that I have no heart, as if yours pulses all the more purely.
Does the red of your heart match the flush in the cheeks of a woman
as she faces a journey to England she shouldn't have to take,
swearing to herself it's just sea salt she can feel in her eyes?

Were Mary's eyes azure like the sky as she raised them to heaven
to avoid the gaze of the girl at her feet convulsing in guilt?
The girl lying in red as she died of the shame she thought she must feel.

Don't tell the doctors they will have blood on their hands
if they try to save a woman at the price of her child.
Don't see another woman tied down by her body,
chained with the law as her blood turns against her.

Don't tell me that you are fighting for the children
while turning away as they died in their thousands
calling them angels and planting them
dead into dirt that you dare call a garden.

There is nothing holy about a lost hole in the ground.

Don't pretend you've forgotten the laundries
where women like us washed their hands of those lives,
where women like us washed linen for their lives,
where women like us lost their whole lives.

Tell me, what do you think of the blood on your hands?

There's blood on our hands and we can't wash it away
with holy water or by swimming the Irish Sea.

So let the blood on our hands be from fighting
for the women we've lost and the women we lose every day.

~ Alice Kinsella

There is No Place

There is no place ...
for debate ...
upon this land
that is
...
my body.
inside, this womb
that I grew
housed.
within me.
mine.
there is no place
for your opinions
to spew
for what you thought you knew about me
there is only one thing
true
this body is mine.

there is no place
for laws and boundaries
borders drawn in the sand
of what part of my body I can own,
and what is governed by a man.

I am the master of this body.
only I have lived this body.
only I know what I am capable of.

this body is mine.

this womb is mine.
these eggs are mine

free to bleed into my sheets. Free to bleed into my hand.
this fetus is mine
free to raise, or choose another time.

For some, there's exclusions
reasons they'll accept
'maybe she was raped,' they'll nod
'maybe this was incest'
but all lives are valid, they say
equal?
well, that's not true
because one life can't live without the other
and I'm the one it's living through.

this body is mine.
it stands here, all on its own
I can't make these babies by myself
it takes a partner, that, I'm sure you know.

there is nothing to debate
no new laws to be signed
this is between myself and doctor
of what medical route they will find
to ease the suffering
of myself, my body, my mind

a medical procedure –
I hope you'll need not find.

and if you so do,
I'll support you in ways you need
no questions, no judgement, absolutely guaranteed.

only you know what's best for you
and I
what's best for me
trust me to my decisions
set the 8th amendment free.

~ Erin Darcy

For all our Heartbeats

For the catch in the throats of people
opening up for the first time
to strangers on their own doorsteps
about the events of their lives,
for the floodgates of stories flowing
from women in their eighties who skivvied in England
avoiding the laundries,
for the bent spine of the man who said,
years ago I would have felt different
but we raised three daughters and I couldn't be prouder
and now I take my direction from them not the clergy
and my wife has passed on but she'd agree with me
she lost her sister to an ectopic pregnancy
and some kind of codology
that said there should be no intervention.

For the grown up wild girls now in their seventies
who we meet on the doorsteps
and for their eye glints and mischief
that have outlasted years of repression;
I'm yes they tell us, yes,
it's high time Ireland got over itself
lord knows it'd be different if men could get pregnant
and for the silence of their generation of men
who seem to be saying nothing about anything
even though they were there
with their brylcream for the show bands and romance,
we're out for them too and their freedom

even if they don't realise it,
we're out for Ann Lovett, who used to shout
on the streets at night time
'come on Granard, wake up.'

We're out for an end to the bitterness and judgement
that doesn't do Ireland justice
and we're out for the young mother
down a country lane at dusk
with her curly haired girl in her arms
who said, I went to Holland myself and I've never told anyone,
I'd postnatal depression and I just couldn't do it
and I swear if we don't win it –
this one won't grow up here
it's cruel in the airport, cruel in the hotel
and worse when you get back
and have to keep your mouth buttoned
as if you've done something shameful
when you did all you could do
and all I can tell you is win lose or draw
my daughter won't live like that.

For the man from Egypt who told us
that his wife is pregnant and he fears for her safety
and has saved money up so they can leave
if she has any complications,
he doesn't understand it because clearly
a woman is more than a foetus
even a fool can see that and for the women
out with us who walked this path in the 80s
and are still here doing it
and can't believe that no one is spitting

for these women who are nervously allowing themselves
to start believing that this time we might win it
we can't let them down.

For the farmer on his tractor
giving us a thumbs up when he sees our jackets
and saying good luck to ye
I've seen cows treated better
than my wife was in pregnancy,
it'll be a yes from me,
for the parents we're meeting whose views
were discounted by doctors and consultants
as if they were spectators who couldn't be trusted
with labour or babies
or being in control of their choices
for the women who've told us they've lost ovaries
and fallopian tubes and had cesarian sections
they didn't consent to.

For the horrors we still have
of children impregnated by relatives
make no mistake we have seen the closed curtains
and for that one young man voting yes
in a house full of no voters
whose eyes welled up when we called
and gave him the chance to tell us
I'm voting with you guys
and for the young people out in their droves
with us to knock on the doors
because we've raised them for better;
Ireland, it's complicated
but we won't give up on you

this time it's got to be yes
because all of our hearts beat
and we don't deserve less.

~ Sarah Clancy

What They Never Said About Love

The loudest word is love
Yelled red-face angrily
Over low bowed heads

Love
Like he said
You remember
Just like he said
Like that, but better
More precise
Sharper
Love

On signs held sideways
By sweat-knuckled hands
Letters smeared in bile
But really love, you see?

It starved sinful babies
Sank their bodies deep
Broke children in the dark
Choked them with silence

He said love, sure he did
But what he meant
What he really meant
Was this

And when it all erupts
In a sudden clutch of cells
Worth forever more than you
Then love is suddenly
Far too small a room

Please await to die
Or cross a cold horizon
A life let fall and break
Because of all the love

But the other love
That one cleared back
Has buds and sap
A wild thing growing

Grafted to bodies
Slipping out of scars
Climbing tiny corpses
To a sun so long forgotten

A love that won't forgive
The things it's seen

A love that's not the silence
But the scream

~ Paddy Kelly

Letters to my Sister

I feel lacking in some kind of permission writing this, having never myself had an abortion. While much of the stories that I and other people tell about my life involve varying degrees of what ex-boyfriends, in their varying degrees of generosity, sympathy, attraction or affection have called recklessness or louchness, this is one area where I have been absolutely strict and controlling.

I often think about this bit of an O'Hara poem in terms of how I experience my own life:

> I have been to lots of parties
> and acted perfectly disgraceful
> but I never actually collapsed
> oh Lana Turner we love you get up

Some withdrawals (accidental pun – sorry!) from what I have just said: what a collapse might be is subjective and differ in severity, Lana Turner can get up. For me here it means I haven't had a baby or a serious or incurable STD. I definitely have collapsed before in many other ways, and often at parties. Sometimes I'm more Lana Turner than Frank O'Hara, but then he could be many things. & for all strictness and control I have also been always lucky. I've been on birth control for almost exactly half of my life, since I was sixteen: I have never been an adult not on some kind of hormones to put off my fertility, I wouldn't trust a condom. I don't have any idea what my experience of myself would be like without these hormones. I know hormones do things to you but I have no base from which to judge that. & my sex life necessitates this. I'm writing this from a man's bed in Barcelona while he's out, the only man I've been with I think who insists on using condoms. I find condoms embarrassing, too much of an acknowledgement that you're having sex. For all my public sex positivity I'm cripplingly self-conscious in ways I've learned to hide well. Of course the former is really a reaction to the latter than an opposition. He's more sensible and calmer than me. It's unusual. I wonder how well it means I know myself to know that this will either be very good for me or will be the reason it ends. Or both. I find the intensity of calm men hard to translate. That we don't speak the same language may make it harder for me to find, though I suspect it is there and may be a better intensity for me than the anxious intensity I always fall for.

I can't remember how old I was, perhaps a teenager, when dad said to me that if I got pregnant he didn't want me to have an abortion, that he would bring up the child if I wanted, of course I didn't want and I made sure never to test what now felt even more complicated, as if it wasn't enough already. Dad's lungs don't work properly, a 'severe pre-natal trauma to the internal organs.' Two failed illegal abortions that were the first thing Graham wrote to him about when Dad tracked him down when we were teenagers. So it must have been around then, which would make me 16. The dates make sense. I wonder if Dad said things like that to you too, I think of it as the prerogative of the eldest child but really I don't know, that's just how I imagine our family structure.

It's strange having grandparents that are not your grandparents, the feeling that you should be intimate, or that they probably want intimacy from you, although they are total strangers and I don't often enjoy talking to strangers. Graham said when he visited I was the child that most reminded him of himself, which I think may be the prism through which he saw things. I can sympathize with that, but I didn't like it. It was probably just because of my grades. That strangeness too for Dad when he died, to mourn a father he'd already mourned in abstract and then found in person. & how mum refused to acknowledged that he had lost a father and that could still be real although different from the time before when he lost his other father, the one we called granddad, not by his name. I wonder how you'll respond to this: as a family we've been trained not to talk much about these things, so I feel that I barely know what you think, or how you think about all this, despite our closeness. I deliberately haven't asked you anything, I hope this gives you freedom to chose what you want to say.

&

Dad never had that conversation with me. Maybe he thought me too young, I must have only been 13 when he spoke to you. Probably, as I grew up, he felt it unnecessary. I never received the same attention from men that you effortlessly attracted. I was awkward and self conscious, the most middle child of middle children. I was never very interested in men myself either. I'm still not. Aromantic, borderline asexual. I'm certain he still thinks I'm gay.

I don't know how to feel about that, or about what he said to you, but I'm glad he never said it to me. Not that it would have changed my mind. Carrying a baby to term was not an option I have ever considered. The moment I knew I was pregnant, before I even took the test, I was googling how to go about booking an abortion. If dad had said those words to me as a teen, perhaps I'd have felt some of the guilt that everyone seems to expect I should have.

I'm glad, knowing that, that I never told our parents. I told pretty much everyone else in my life. My boss wished me luck, my friends threw me a party (we watched the abortion episodes of Bojack Horseman and crazy-ex-girlfriend, 'Brrap Brrap, Pew Pew'). I was casual, aggressively casual, about letting everyone know that I wasn't ashamed. I answered my manager's enquiry about my health with 'It's just morning sickness, I'm getting it sorted tomorrow', my coworkers concern about my painkiller use with 'I had an abortion so I'm feeling a bit sore'. But I didn't tell mum and dad.

For them, for dad especially, abortion would have been viewed as a big decision, something traumatic that you shouldn't do without good reason. And, even if mine were good enough, they'd think it something I should be upset and emotional about even considering. I didn't know how I could possibly explain that I wasn't. That I knew the circumstances of Dad's birth, the two attempted illegal abortions, the prenatal trauma, the fact that neither of us would exist if it had worked, and that it didn't factor into my thoughts in any way. For me, there was never any decision involved; any other option was simply unthinkable. But being pro-choice does not mean it is a choice they want to think about their daughters making, and making so easily.

Also, and this is deeply embarrassing, I didn't want to have to explain the how I got pregnant. That I had slept with a guy I wasn't that into, that I had done it because it seemed a more convenient way of getting rid of him than having to deal with the whining if I told him he was nice but I didn't want to see him again. Because I had not had sex or been on a date in forever and I thought I'd give it a try. Experiment with at least acting like I have the libido of a normal functioning adult. Verdict: sex is still not that great.

Unlike you, I have never been on birth control. I say I don't have sex often enough to justify taking hormones, and that's true. My mental health is fragile enough on its own, why would I throw hormones in the mix? But also the one time I raised it with a nurse as a teen, under the convenient excuse of wanting to halt my periods for a one month trip, I was shot down so thoroughly that I never bothered asking anyone for it again. I split up with my boyfriend not long after, and it wasn't like I've had regular sex since.

And, unlike you, I always use a condom. It's the one condition of entry I set. No man had ever ignored that. Every man, however reluctant, respected that. Respected me. Right up until this one thought I wouldn't notice if he slipped it off. Thought that his pleasure was more important than the conditions I had set to my consent. It's taken me a year and a half to acknowledge that for what it clearly is, to accept that if I would call it rape if it happened to someone else, I should have the self respect call it rape when it happens to me.

How would I explain that to mum and dad? 'Yes, I was raped, but I consented to sex'. Could you see mum understanding that? I can't even explain that part to most of my friends. This is the first time you are hearing about it now, and I wonder even as I type whether I should have shared it, I know how furious it will make you.

And how to explain to our parents, to anyone, that the fact that it was a rape did not factor into my decision to abort. To explain that at the time I buried those thoughts and feelings to come to terms with later, because the more pressing issue was that I was pregnant and that I did not want to be. And what more reason than that do I need? An unwanted baby, a complete uprooting of the life I was only just starting to build, a change of circumstance too big to even allow myself to think about, was horrific enough by itself.

It's why the line 'not even in cases of rape, incest or fatal foetal abnormality' still makes me fume whenever I see it, and I've been seeing it a lot recently. As if those three situations (two really, if we consider that most incest is rape) are the only ones a woman, a *good* woman anyway, should ever consider an abortion (nobody but ciswomen gets abortions in these rhetorical debates). 'Not *even*', as if it's perfectly valid to exclude all the other myriad of reasons a woman might not want a baby. Oh, or 'if it threatens the mother's life'. Neat, tragic, reasons that everyone can understand. Reasons that convey the image of a woman who has done all the right things, has all the right motherly instincts, but has been wronged by either men or biology. The good woman is a victim, never an agent. Even in the fight to let women have a choice.

And it's always a 'difficult' choice when we are allowed to make it. 'The hardest decision a woman will ever make'. Another lie I keep hearing. It was the easiest decision of my life. The best decision of my life. Maybe I'm an exception. Maybe I truly am abnormal. Maybe every person but me who's ever had an abortion has agonised over it. But I don't think so. Some have. Many, in fact. Most? I don't know. But there's enough of us that haven't.

All these lines, repeated again and again to demonstrate the pro-life movement as the regressive, misogynist, and backwards stance that it is, are lines that simultaneously shame every woman who's ever had an abortion for the simple, valid, reason that she doesn't want a child. Lines that talk over the lived experiences of the people actually affected. My story wouldn't appeal to the masses. It wouldn't win arguments. Or votes.

I'm not sympathetic.

I could make my story palatable of course, a simple matter of reframing the narrative. I could play up the victimhood, emphasise my singleness, my mental health, my financial situation, the fact that I later discovered the man already had a partner and two children. I could focus on those facts and pretend I would have made a different choice in different circumstances. It's the element mum and dad might need to understand it. But it wouldn't be true. And I refuse to make myself into a passive victim just to make someone else more comfortable.

ॐ

Perhaps I shouldn't have told you that thing about dad, that while for me it was important and I am partly narrativising me to you, for you that is information more unhelpful than helpful. The ethics of honesty are very difficult I think. You don't have any obligation to other people to give them the facts of your life that you are uncomfortable sharing with them and giving them only partial facts of your life is not dishonesty. A relationship of honesty is an interpersonal thing not the responsibility of the person who gives or does not give information. If the relationship does not make it possible to share certain facts, that is not the burden of the person who does not give information, though I think it is often experienced as such. That relationship can be transformed, sometimes, often it cannot. & partiality is an unavoidable foundation of interpersonal relationships. We all narrativize ourselves even to ourselves, we can't fit everything in.

It's hard to work out how to structure this reply; your email has so many pressing urgencies I feel I need to hold onto, but how to do that and still stay structured and comprehensible? I'm sorry, given the subject matter, that you have had a few days of silence, though also I knew this was within the agreed bounds of how this interaction would work and so my feeling was that it would not be uncomfortable for you and you would tell me if it was. But I didn't want to react outside the bounds we had established by sending you a shorter message that wasn't part of the project, where we had decided on a capaciousness that might allow us to process and speak in a particular way. I'm interested in the fact that you feel you maybe shouldn't tell me to protect me from my feelings of fury. Of course I felt fury, but I wonder why you want to protect me from it. I often act on my fury in self-damaging ways: yesterday I'd intended to be writing this but had to spend most of the day drafting apologies for an email sent in fury: though this time a fury at being a 'casual' (read precarious) member of staff in a university department where the permanent members of staff debated whether or not we should have voting rights in departmental decisions and discussed whether or not we were capable of using this vote responsibly. I also know there is a particular group of people – almost exclusively women and it includes you – for whom I will attack far harder than I would for myself if I feel they have been threatened. The man I had to apologize to had bullied one of them and I know that played a part.

In terms of timing, I couldn't let myself engage fully with the feelings incurred by your email when I was a guest in someone else's house, it would have made me a terrible guest, I needed to think alone. I'm home now.

I'm not going to offer you my fury, and that is perhaps helpful in me processing it healthily in this particular situation. And if you are trying to protect me from it you perhaps don't want it. And I have more furies: at the judgment of sexual health clinics and the kind of conditioning which means you and me and so many people I know have had sex with another person because it's easier than dealing with them being pissed off with you for not, and that we are then the ones that also suffer embarrassment at that decision.

Yes Dad did think you were gay! I remember him explaining to me once that he was pretty sure that the reason you were depressed was because you were gay and couldn't accept yourself or were worried about the acceptance of others. I laughed, which to him perhaps seemed callous, but I knew more than him. For starters I knew you weren't gay, but that is always the explanation for women who are not normative in that particular way in their dating patterns. I wasn't normative the other way, so I always identified with 'whores', what my friend Rachel gave me a word for, *homo sacer*, the man (though here woman and therefore already differently socially configured) 'set apart'. (S)he is banned & may be killed by anybody, though not as a sacrifice. The unassimilatable.

One of the things I think about often: that moment in *Lady and the Tramp* when the Peggy Lee dog sings. And you get that she's a tramp too, though she's not allowed to be as trampish as the male tramp, she has her heart broken, is not the heartbreaker, in the story she

55

tells, and she's so much more alive and exciting than Lady, who is your classic mild girl-woman in dog form. Peggy Lee is a sexy mongrel and knows it, not an acceptable form of breed-type. Lady will be allowed to leave the pound soon, she doesn't 'belong there', that's clear, and when she's done singing Trixie sashays back into her cell.

How to walk as if you're free though you can't leave the prison. Though the sashaying sexy woman is I find also a prison. Perhaps I should have paid more attention to what she was saying. I'd prefer to break down the prison.

Right at the beginning of *The Scarlet Letter*, another touchstone text for me, Hawthorne says

> The founders of a new colony, whatever Utopia of human virtue they might they might originally project, have invariably recognized it among their earliest practical necessities to allot a portion of the virgin soil as a cemetery, and another portion as the site of a prison.

Hester emerges from the prison wearing the sign of the prison. A. The first letter. So we're told.

The attraction bit is easy for me, I suppose, though learned uneasily. What goes along with it is not. Though there's a lot of joy in this. & re: normal. Fuck normal. I used to examine myself every day for signs that I was abnormal. I had no idea of what a normal was to make this judgment from. One thing that I feel bonds us quite strongly is that we both have non-normative sexualities, though what that non-normativity is is the polar opposite. But it creates commonality and sympathy between us rather than feeling opposite. At least I find.

Back to my laughter. It was more than this though, it was the sense of there being a simple explanation that could explain, be found to be the source, of this thing he really wanted to be able to solve away. When I was anorexic he was relieved – though it seems odd to say it – that it could be seen to have a cause in my being raped at 14. Again, I don't really call it rape to myself, though I suppose whatever the forms of my not really feeling capable of asserting a refusal to someone my being 14 and him 32 establishes not only some of the reasons why I couldn't but also the definitions of the event as an act of rape.

Of course it wasn't just this, this itself was a product of something already happening, the way I feel I'd already been taught that sex was shameful so was actively seeking it out in acts of rebellion that left me unable to put any care for myself into my actions. If it is already shameful why would you take care of yourself. One of the cruelest things our culture does to teenagers I think is teach them that their bodies and sexualities are shameful and not to be spoken of right at the time that they become a pressing matter so you must navigate these necessary developments as acts of insubordination.

Anyway, this explanation seemed to satisfy people so this is what I told the therapist and having given them what I presumed they wanted I allowed myself to not go back to the therapist and instead go to the nutritionist, where I could make lists of all the foods I ate, which was what I was actually interested in. Obviously there is an obsessiveness around self-control in there, which sits perfectly, I think, though may seem not to, with my recklessness. I can conform, self-control and rebel; it's hard to find healthier options, though I'm getting there. & taking up space, that much cited feminist-issue. I always blame mum for all of this, the way she wanted my difficult emotions and sexuality, to just disappear so that we would all be ok. I disappeared a lot of myself. But families are cultural units and exist to an extent to indoctrinate us into the culture that produces them as the useful unit. It's interesting that we were both anorexic and both have very little desire towards creating a family. Sometimes the terms of Claire's existence seem so opposed to ours I wonder how to engage. But you were always closer to her than me. I saw myself as the awkward middle too, navigating, as I remember things, the constant battles between mum and dad on one side and you and Claire on the other, though also I was always Dad's ally in this, trying to keep life tolerable enough for him that he wouldn't leave. I think in the absence of being able to tell mum about anything – the thing we all feel – I became the repository of the things that he couldn't say to mum, that's why I think him saying those sorts of things to me is symptomatic of my being the eldest, though I think your interpretation, too, holds.

My anorexia was partly a refusal of sex, in my mind it protected me from my boyfriend at the time trying to sleep with me, but it wasn't like rape was an originary trauma, it had already been prepared for. Even in my sexual activity around this at the time, the fact that I was sleeping with my best friend and I found her attempts to continue having sex coercively pushed me far beyond the bounds of what I was comfortable with much more traumatic at the time. I'd already learned that I didn't have the power to assert the desires of my body over other people's desires for it. I think I've been a people-pleaser from a very young age, in my narrative of our childhoods I am always the emissary in the fights of the family until I became a teenager and started to cause them.

The popular representation of psychology would have you understand revelation as cure. There's a book by Stephen Grosz, a not-so-poppy psychoanalyst where he writes up narratives of particular therapy cases. They all end with a moment of revelation, and understanding of why something is happening in the present because of a past event repressed or not fully understood previously. This really should be only part of a story, not its conclusion. I found the book useful, and had lots of revelations. Which is to say its premise is flawed: there are slow accumulations of linked causes, sometimes manifested in events and learning to link them up is only a foundation point for further action.

To me this relates to what you are 'meant to feel' about having an abortion: that it is a seismic event. I'm pretty sure, beyond the fact that it's physically painful and requires (unnecessarily I would say, is this deliberate I wonder?) huge amounts of planning and effort, it wouldn't be a decision I would hesitate or dwell on either. Other than that I don't see it as much different to taking the morning-after pill and I would never not do this if there was any risk and I never think much about it afterwards. It's very easy to single out particular things – like what you've decided constitutes life and ignore all of the other things that are linked to this. Anti-abortionists so often pro-the right to bear arms, or climate change deniers, endangering actual human lives but only indirectly, at a distance where they don't have to think about it. Last week as I was writing to you I took a course of antibiotics that killed the bacteria inflaming my bladder. And there are many things that could have happened that would mean we, and Dad, wouldn't exist. People could have had sex at a different time; someone could have done too much cycling and reduced their sperm count. Our bodies mean we're forced into having the decisions we always already make without considering their implications, and the chances that already occur made things that become pressing for us to consider.

I've been avoiding the largest event of your email, I thought because I felt I had nothing to offer except saying that I'm sorry that happened to you, and performances of fury. I know we live in a world where even talking through forms of justice is a futile act of rage. But I think it might be more than that: I don't know what I want to people to say to me. I don't want to tell a story where I've been raped and people say sorry that that happened to you afterwards. I want to be able t tell it as a thing in my life among others, not the main event. There are so many things that are more important. And that reaction undoes what the point of telling the story was, that it became about an ability to tell a story and be an agent in diagnosing and transforming your world, not being someone who has had something bad happen to you. And it's important, I think, to think of these things not as singular or defining events, but as particular heightened moments of our everyday. I liked the way you did this and how we are doing some of this together.

&

My turn to apologise to you for leaving this too long, for making you wait several days for a reply. I imagine I felt much like you must have when you read my email, my mind stopping at certain phrases, unable to move past these new facts they reveal. Facts that, in hindsight, I should have been aware of already. It has taken me until today to be able to read this and take it in as it was intended, to focus on the message in your words and not those new facts I now need to insert into the narrative of our childhoods.

I have a lot of thoughts, and I'm not entirely sure how to express them, but I will not say 'sorry that that happened to you'. That wasn't why you shared your story, and it wasn't why I shared mine. Any performances of fury I might want to make against any one person or another would be almost twenty years too late. And as unhelpful to you as I find other peoples performances of fury on my behalf.

Instead, I shall continue to be furious with a wider society that continues to offer women no respect or understanding when it comes to issues of sex, consent, and bodily autonomy but all of the judgement when those are abused.

~ Katharine Peddie

The Hag the Witch
the Pagan Bitch

Síle Na Gig

Ireland had the cradle held,
by hook and hammer horn,
an ancient place where freedom sparked a fire from a thorn.
Ireland spoke with bitter breath a lemon spittle curd,
all dancing ceased so too the feast ... the Síle Na Gig was born.

Her stony gaze is warmer than a Sunday Mass in June,
you can hear the silent whisper that scratches at her womb,
"The Hag the witch the pagan bitch, The awful lustful whore."
So pushed she was through rusty gates she enters so forlorn.
But when judgement came, compassion left and locked every single door.

And now she beats her tightened drum to sound the crack of dawn.
Arise! Arise! my sleepless ones come hear this brand new sound.
She screams ... Repeal the 8th from church and state and let never more
    be said,
that Irish girls with ragged curls will board that lonely plane.
And finally we lay to rest the shame and needless loss,
since '83 the bigotry was at every woman's cost.

                                              ~ Stephanie Hough

This Time

Give her a choice.

Give her a voice in a country that sings songs of freedom on an unbalanced equilibrium between men and women.

Give her power, don't just make her a number on a list of expectant mothers. Where there was no other way, no other path, forced to accept the fact that society sees her as a vessel. Something that may carry life but never live it. Something that, when attacked, must accept it, forget it and move on, be strong for the baby's sake.

Men take her body and write down what parts are hers and she is cursed by the ink in their very pens. Her future decided there and then, again by an oppressed nation.

Give her love, it is her nature. Don't make her a murderer when her life is endangered, when her mind is a stranger that left long ago, when she pleaded no and he let himself go on top of her.

Give her a cure in a time that only treats symptoms.

Give her a say in whether our future will be compiled of broken children. An echoing era of repetition where religion still dictates a woman's place in this world.

Give her back what's hers. Her body. Her first and foremost right in this life.

Because all of her life she's been given Nos.

No you can't dress like that.

No you can't do a job like that.

No you can't earn as much.

Live as much.

Matter as much.

No.

No you can't say no.

No. You can't grow any bigger. Go any further. You won't be considered for the position because you might just end up a mother. No.

So give her your help. She can't do this alone when no is all she's ever known.

So this time, give her yes.

~ Lizzy Byrne

A Lucky One

The morning after
she walks home from his,
her only wish to sleep starfished
in her own bed.
Fine to share for a night,
but nothing long term now.
See she's a BA,
MA all out of the way,
and on, she can't wait.

But then

it's late.

One Sunday morning wakes
and takes another look at a clean white pad,
realises she'd had those
sickly morning warning signs,
and finds her way to the chemist.

Heads back under a Clearblue sky
and wonders, why?
She was safe, she thought.
But who knows when it was bought,
kept in a wallet, wearing thin.

She begins to cry.
Books a flight
away for a night
to visit long lost Aunt Marie.
She's a lucky one.
What about the one who, fifteen,
left her school hall to make that laboured crawl to the grotto.

Or the one who can't feed the three she has.
She's short for the weekly shop,
forget that costly hop across to get
the care that she needs.

Or the one who's a refugee,
can't leave so left to see
her child receive
direct provision life

as one of our twelve a day
sent Ryanair's way.
Sure, she's exiled.
She's shunned.

But she's a lucky one.

~ Saoirse Anton

Wake Up

Don't cross your legs like that,
or curl them under you, like a cat.
That's no way for a lady to behave.
See the state, not you,
knows best what to do
with your body
from cradle to grave.

With faux Christian guise,
pulling wool over eyes,
they drive woman after woman away.
Whether certain or scared
we just wish our state cared
that with our wombs
we want our own say
So it's time that we vote,
to save more from the boat.
We all will be equal one day.
With strength and with faith,
we'll repeal the Eighth.
Wake up Ireland,
we're coming your way.

~ Saoirse Anton

A Beauty Uncivilised

Lissadell you cast Sligeach spells
Of Fenian heights and glory writes
With sunset showers of daffodils
Casting shadows on Connacht knights
Here every Greek knook Counts
Echoing the stills of Ireland's gazelles
100 years of tears that mounts
A beauty uncivilised sounding bells
Adorned with Alpine gardens of delights
Running us away to Sligo bay
As the evening light casts aflight
Where kimonos whisper for us to stay
Lissadell, you countess wrap us warm
Hold us steady as all around we feel
Wave that patriot flag as born
Bring the silhouettes of Medb and Bulben to knell
We rise in you, Sligeach grá glue
Bless, we will, we did see this through
As the witch hunters try to scald
This new femina dawn will rise has risen unwalled

~ Lisa Dee

71

Spindle Pricked, the Fly Forages for its Resin: A Fable from a Moonless Land

Driving the old woman home with lurch and bump,
the fly does not inquire about her laundry – dirty or no –
but does stop off to sleep for a hundred years.

Awake at last, the fly hears the old woman's twelfth
child – the one she raises for penance – partaking of toast
and tea. Thick air undulates against the window panes

and the fly rubs her eyes red trying to see the castle
in the brambles, but there is only a shred of nylon staked
out on elastic bands. Sinewy, the black bears circle,

and the fly, grown large with import, challenges one
to a duel. The bear's gauntlet is made of slain sled dogs,
the very pups who dared howl at the midnight sun.

Dual? scoffs the bear, Sheridan's lectures peeping from
her sleeved fawn waistcoat. First blood drawn, the fly aims to
delope, but the damn resin makes the fire stick. Just so

she rubs her jointed legs along her swollen abdomen, her
salivary glands set alight. With this softening, the body yields
at last to its chosen fate. The carrion is ready, the death

all life portends. The resin hardens, and heliotropic
trees bow low, know smiles. The old woman nods sagely,
having swallowed many flies, and the odd bear too.

～ Sara Crangle

What Stories Will Tell Us
& Our Lives?

thou

I stumbled upon myself. I gathered wholesomely into one solid being, like a clump of trees, grounded. Self-contained, self-aware. I tripped over my own reflection when he looked into my eyes. Solidness painted my/*thou*/soul in one thick brush stroke, across his landscape. I stumbled into my womb, suddenly with its own rhythm. Self-contained, self-aware.

When the seed was planted.

I held myself against my flexed legs, containing *thou* skin and bones, and this breath, this breath of warmth. A human volcano, activated. The plate tectonics shifting-moving-flowing, in no order but in chaos. Initially my head was down, breathing into the crevices between my heart cage and the bend legs, as if de-guttering the channels of flow. Lastly the door of *thou* mouth opened towards the ceiling of the cube of the yellow of a reality. The vapour of heated shock melted upwards despite the grave gravity, a sound broke through from the tip of the alveoli, just because its distance, just because its depth, just because the strong impulse to let the sound of heated shock out of this inner world, of this inner displacement.

Termination – *thou* need to terminate. To not want to terminate. For it to be no option ... but ... to terminate. For it to not be an option to terminate. Consequence. Balance consequence.

The situation, was. Yes, I approved first and Yes, I approved second. But to second was fearsome, no frisson involved but gutting, disjointing, deconstructing, turning the wheel of fortune backwards.

I stumbled upon my shadow, it looked whole and complete, after second happened. No holes, or gaps of see through light, no evidence of stitches of fate. We humans have several substances, not just soul and body, but temporal, timeless – substances.

I ate *thou* self, inside out, thoughts carved though brain lobes, feelings painted out reality, dendrites shooting pain towards sunset.

The situation is –
a blank new sheet. The harvest of seeds to be placed back in the ground. Fertility proved.

~ Lucia Sellars

The Birth of Rain

My body is charred
and red, from holding you.
I sit on the wing
of a plane,
my dignity as my carry-on
and the weight of judgement
checked into the hold.

The heat of this
evening
is so still, so close.
With its breath sucked out
and squeezed
like a deflated lemon.

Foreigners look at my eyes,
and see me wince.
Blue in the evening,
black at night,
my tears – colourless, salty,
and procedural.

I feel my shape
shift – ever so slightly,
and the passage of life

is as significant as
my money, my pride,
my choice.

When rain clouds gather,
and, pregnant,
send sparks across the sky
tumultuous winds howl.
They moan across towns
and villages that wait,
poised.

With the weight lifted
off me now, my heart bursts out
in song, in memory
of freedom.
As I take off.

Today, the air is fresh,
clean and blowy.
And my head is held high
because it is okay
to want as I want today.

And there is no need for
the birth of rain.

~ Udita Banerjee

Deconstruction

I saw you emerge as a rat
in white plaster dust shining
your eyes and nose up towards me

I saw you chew over the joist
suck out the juice from the backbones
and leave a small pile of twigs on the table
which I cleared away

Behind the skirting board you found
a mummified rat
spread-eagled in desiccation
only a wind dried duck in the window
of a Chinese restaurant
but grey as a crevice

Later it dangled in the car window
'How could you' I said
as we passed Kew Gardens
'My aunt used to take me to the Chinese pavilion'
you replied
'I asked her why all the steps were broken
 and she said that my uncle had done it'

When we came back Rentokil stood
on the doorstep

It was a warm sunny morning in April

The formalities take a long time when your mouth is dry and no one said, as he had said, 'It won't be as bad as you think'. They asked for the money with an apologetic smile and I handed across the carefully prepared pile of notes, 50% his and 50% mine. We were led off to a ward where we complained of the dryness, the terrible thirst and, for some, the terrible hunger. Told to put on ugly white operation robes, we helped each other tie them at the back. Giving two Valium pills as a pre-med the nurse apologised for making us swallow them without water. 'I bet these knock you out.' Arm bands had been stuck onto us with three numbers and we decided that one represented our age, another the ward and the third the order in which we would be led off to the operation. 'It's just like a conveyer belt.' Quick nods of agreement from the other beds. We settled down and grew silent. The Valium had little effect. I was taken to a small room, lay down and saw the masked anaesthetist and his nurse. I still had a mark on my arm from a blood sample and said 'I hope you make a better injection than the last person did.' He smiled, the nurse asked my name and the needle entered my arm. I remember coming back to consciousness, vibrating and swollen, clutching at the steel bars of a cot, crying, 'Please ... Please.' I tried to focus on the face of a nurse, two inches from mine, who was shouting 'Don't make so much noise. You'll upset the other patients.' Bundled into a wheelchair I was taken back to the ward. When we were all in our beds the nurse explained that we would probably want to go to the toilet but that feeling was due to the rectum being pressed down during the operation and would go away.

A wife and mother had taken a low dosage contraceptive which didn't work. She had no desire for more children and her previous pregnancies had been difficult. She hadn't told the children where she was going but lied and said she was going on a course. 'They might be funny about it. They might not like it.' During her pregnancy she had to carry on working although she was often tired and sick. The children complained that she always went to bed very early and took less interest in them. An English courier, living with a Spaniard, found her work demanding and poorly paid and its main advantage was the chance to live in Spain. When she became pregnant she visited a doctor who warned her against termination because of a cyst in her vagina, but the doctor in England could find no trace of such a cyst. Abortion was impossible in Spain and her travel company had already made use of this London clinic. Her boss suggested she take some of the firm's publicity stickers to put in the clinic window. The next day she would catch a company plane back to work. After the operation, before the pain had worn off, she said, 'I'll make him pay for this.' A quiet, shy girl from Durham was making her first visit to London. Her boyfriend had been opposed to the abortion – they were to be married in a year's time – but she felt that it was wrong to start their married life with a child they had not planned. They were saving for a house and she was sure that to have a child now would be the wrong way to start their lives together. A French Assistante cried a little and slept some of the time. She said nothing about the man who had made her pregnant and had told no one of her situation, not even her flat-mate.

Some women came in from another ward and they were all Irish. A seventeen-year-old had been heavily pregnant and obliged to pay the higher fee for the abortion. Her girl friend had found the money. When they crossed the Irish sea, they were stopped by the police, who suspected she was running away from home but allowed her to go on after she made a phone call to her parents. She was a nurse and hoped to find work in England. She told us her story, sitting on the edge of the bed, smoking, showing no sign that she'd had a more serious operation than the rest of us.

....

When we got home the man from Rentokil was waiting to be let in. It was a warm, sunny morning in April.

From a journal, 1980.

~ Frances Presley

One Sings, the Other Doesn't:
A Reproductive Rights Muscial for the Moment

It's 1972, but it's not. It's 1977, and it's a film. It's 2018, and the film is re-released.

Agnès Varda's *One Sings, the Other Doesn't* is the story of two friends whose lives are connected, and shaped, by access to abortion and what Varda, on a recent visit to London, called 'self-control of birth.' Some years after middle-class schoolgirl Pauline (aka Pomme) helps a young woman who lives in her building raise the funds to travel to Switzerland for an abortion, they meet again at a (famous) 1972 protest outside the courtroom in Bobigny, a commune in the northeastern suburbs of Paris. Pomme sings, Suzanne doesn't: it's Pomme's voice that leads Suzanne (now a health worker) forward through the crush to the barricades to find her friend standing on a bollard.

Pomme relates her own story of travelling to Amsterdam for an abortion, a flashback that also shows Pomme writing her first song, a jaunty number about taking a canal trip with a group of fellow abortees, and includes a lingering shot of the vacuum aspirator in the clinic. Later in the film, Suzanne hosts a consciousness-raising session about contraception at her small-town clinic, leading to a lively discussion; one also follows Pomme's performance when she visits, questioning the essentialism of some of her lyrics. And Pomme (demonstrating how to get a latch when breastfeeding) tells her husband Darius that, if he wants to return to Iran, they will just

85

have to have *two* children together, and raise one each in their countries of origin.

One Sings still stands out in the history of cinema for its frank address to both the politics and practicalities of reproductive rights – it's hard to think of another film that addresses abortion as anything other than a moral judgement or personal crisis, and even more rare to find a film that combines the informative with the affective in presenting the right to choose. Without simplification or sloganeering (well, there are placards – and a song that quotes Engels), it weaves the history of the struggle for reproductive rights in France into a tale of friendship, motherhood and professional becoming, paralleling Pomme's and Suzanne's work as much as their intimate and familial lives.

Varda herself was on the barricades in 1972. She signed the *Manifeste de 343* alongside Simone de Beauvoir, Françoise Sagan, Catherine Deneuve, Marguerite Duras and other well-known French women, declaring that they had had abortions. She assisted women who had clandestine abortions before 1975, providing the use of her house on the Rue Daguerre, where she was raising two children. And, when it came to making the film, she cleverly wove together this historical experience with the fictional tale of two friends. Members of the Mouvement pour le libération des femmes (MLF) appear as extras – and the film received MLF certification! The curly-haired lawyer pushing through the barricades with Suzanne is (played by) Gisèle Halimi, the lawyer who won the Bobigny case, a precedent that led to the introduction of the Veil law legalizing early-term medical abortion in 1975, where the film concludes.

30 June 2018: Simone Veil is interred in the Panthéon, only the fifth woman to be accorded the honour by the Republic. 5 July 2018: *One Sings, the Other Doesn't* is re-released nationwide in France (it's touring the UK this summer via Club des Femmes' *Revolt, She Said: Women and Film After '68* programme), after the film's

86

restoration premiered on the beach at the 2018 Cannes Film Festival. The worth of neither Veil nor Varda is defined by the (foot-dragging) shift of states and soft power actors towards a liberal vision of equality, but a mo(ve)ment is nevertheless palpable. Although *One Sings* was commercially successful on its original 1977 French release, it was critically mocked for its luscious, witty musical approach to a political subject (by radical feminists, who felt it wasn't serious enough) and for considering that women and domestic issues were worthy of attention (by mainstream critics). *One Sings, the Other Doesn't*: the film itself knows that both approaches to life (including motherhood – or not), and to political struggles, are valid, and need each other.

'They'd fought,' says the voice-over at the film's conclusion (delivered by Varda herself, over an image of her daughter Rosalie Varda playing Suzanne's daughter), 'to gain the happiness of being a woman.' It's a radical and powerful take on de Beauvoir's adage: 'a woman is not born, nor made, but fought for.' Varda said in London that she had found friendships and happiness at protests; perhaps there is (under heteropatriarchal colonial capitalism) no fully-realised non-dominant subject position that is possible without participation in the struggle, whether sign-wielding, singing, or running a clinic. It's 2018, and we're still fighting. And we still have Pomme and Suzanne on our side.

~ So Mayer

A Statistically Average Day in Early 21st Century Ireland

Chloe wakes,
Hello Kitty flashing five as dawn breaks,
stomach flat, tummy aches
for a cup of tea, she takes
nil by mouth, her mam fakes
a smile. She's doing this for both their sakes.

Sinéad kisses the twins
goodbye!
She doesn't, but they cry.
A mile to the bus, a sigh
as she sits, considering sins
and missed pills and why
her?

Laura hails
the taxi and passes the note,
the address that she wrote
so carefully, her nails
digging into her hands as he notes it, she fails
to avoid his eye but he smiles and sails
through the traffic. He's heard the tales.

Mary fidgets, waits.
It's thick and tense and she absolutely hates
the silence.
She waits.
And misses her gang, they're twelve, ten, and eight,
and ah sure they're great
but
she was finished.
She is finished.
She no longer creates, her uterus lying in state, she abdicates.
She does not leave this up to the fates.

Michelle stands in the gallery door.
Be careful what you wish for.
A city break, a day
off
but back to the clinic by four,
Cinderella leaving a piece of herself on the floor.
Conor is two and Emma almost four.
She absolutely cannot do any more
than she's doing.

Sarah surfaces from
dark.
It's done.
Her heart
in her chest.

The nurse calls her love.
The tears come
Sorry, I'm sorry, I'm just
It's done.

Lisa grips
her armrests, hips
pressed back in the seat, she waits for the ding.
Seatbelt sign off, she springs
up, bathroom, cramped, cramps, drips.
She's used to trips
but this –
Back in her seat, neat, reviewing scripts,
work in the morning. Biting her lips.

Niamh pulls in
the narrow lane, the light wanes.
She's drained.
Closes the hall door on the rain
her sister draws her in.
They open the envelope, the treasure obtained.
One blister's already been
opened, the others for later, then the pain
offered, profane.

Emma doesn't know
so she checks, the glow
of her phone,
You have visited this site 21 times
She's alone.
How much blood is too much blood?
She told her housemates she had to go.
A 'funeral.' RIP Great Aunt Flo.
How much blood do I have?
She wants to call her parents, no
she wants to call her sister. *Hello*
I'm after having a wee abortion
How much is too much?
No.
She's alone.

Cathy climbs the stairs,
he's there,
her baby boy, her only child, her fair-haired
world.
Asleep, with his bear,
a day of daycare and his aunt, not a care.
The loss, the despair
doesn't touch him, she dares
to hope it never will. She aches for a pair.
She needs to share
her love with two, her prayers

were not answered. The spot, the scare
Incompatible with life.
Beyond unfair.
Her tiny tragedy. She tears
herself away, to wash her hair,
wash away the whole affair –
as if she ever could.

~ Emer Ellis-Neenan

Author's note. This poem was composed from the statistics of
those who travel every day from Ireland: their ages, their
reasons, their existing children, and even their names describe
the statistical averages. Data was drawn from the Irish Family
Planning Association, the UK Department of Health and
Social Care, Johnston's Archive, and the Central Statistics
Office of Ireland.

I Have a Friend

I have a friend, let's call her Jill.
Who found out she was pregnant despite being on the pill.
The man in the transaction said he didn't want to know.
So she took a plane to England where the desperate have to go.
I have a friend, let's call her Sue,
had a grown-up family and a dying Dad too,
a Mum who needed help and a 50th birthday looming,
found herself pregnant but didn't find herself blooming.
I have a friend, let's call her Geri,
who started to miscarry on the Liverpool ferry.
She didn't need the consult but she still had to pay the fee
and then bled home in a toilet on the Irish Sea.
I have a friend, let's call her Jan,
got told a horror story at a sixteen-week scan.
She didn't live in Ireland and so didn't have to leave
with compassion and with heartbreak she could stay at home to grieve.
I have a friend, let's call her you.
May you never have to face what a million others do.
But if it comes to pass, then the only wish I give
is that you can access what you need in the country where you live.
We all have friends, they are sisters, they are mothers.
They are girlfriends, they are wives. They have fathers. They have
    brothers.

We should trust them with their lives, help to mitigate their stress
By simply standing in their shoes to tick the box for yes.
Thanks, you.

~ Maria Haughey

10 Telechirics in
Anticipation of the Vote

*

Stirring porridge to overseas radio accompaniment, I am hearing one Irish doctor speak of 'the difficulty medical professionals have in defining where a threat to health becomes a threat to life.'[i] This medic is weighing her every syllable as she explains: that the environment born of the current legislation carries risks 'particularly relating to the timing of critical clinical decision-making in saving a woman's life'[ii]; that there arise *problems* (death-ly ones) due to 'over-emphasis on the need not to intervene until the foetal heartbeat stopped.'[iii] And I could vomit into that pot but instead, knowing there are months more of this ahead, before a referendum might happen, might maybe be passed, I keep on stirring. Trouble.

*

Taking an early morning flight between these two countries, I am arrested anew by the thought of how my movements register in the context of Ireland's particular model of offshoring. The onenight wheeliebag of a woman of a certain age making a brief stopover, alone. Scanning the queue, I accidentally smile in wellmeaning mortification at any woman, un-equally alone, who probably didn't come across just to do a lecture.

*

Rules govern media engagement on this so-contested uteral turf. All rallies must receive equal coverage. When voices collide on radio, there is only so much time that can be apportioned to compassion, before it must cede to hatred. Hourglasses must be tipped on the handover between each speaker and the next. Is this Adorno's fear, right here? His faith in the power of the satingloved voice that could insinuate itself right into your reason by route cochlear?

In the grain of this presenter's delivery: her clockwatching frustration. Fear of bias, of backlash, of the lawyers set loose at a sniff of <impartiality>. Hackles perma-erect, defenders of the right to deny the right surge from leashes that can be cut by any breach of policy and they circle round us even here. Over the swallowing of my breakfast, the internal soundscape of my own body, I can hear them, howling.

'The second complaint in relation to the abortion issue concerned the use of the word "abortion."'[iv]

*

Take me to a changing room and I'll point out the convent girls, by the way they might move. All those who were listening hard when the priest intoned: 'But the angel assured her, "Mary, you have nothing to fear. God has a surprise for you."'[v]

We call now before us all who feared that they too might, to their surprise, become blessed amongst women. I want to survey those woolly vested virgins: the girls who shut their eyes against a beam of April sun through stained glass; lest it should reveal itself as a Sign: th'augur that would align them with their destiny. If they have found ways, by now, to reside inside their own bodies, I will hug them to my unprepossessing bosom. As for the rest, I wave from inside my modesty towel, carefully.

And though others of my acquaintance have recalled being equally beset by this most catholic worry, not once have I been told by a friend that she had done this thing we were being trained to think unthinkable. The older I get, the sadder the silence.

*

Instead, I grew up hearing radiosnatches about the finding of unavowable offspring, alive and dead. And of their mothers, children still, pushed 'down through the social oubliette,'[vi] their unmarried bodies—denounced, criminalised, sectioned—unclaimed by any sire; they must have been the sites of so many immaculate conceptions.

*

Polymerpocalypse aside, I'm doubly glad that plastic bags are so much less in (ab)use now. That there are so many fewer about to snag in ditches, and billow, ominously.

Because even as an adult, seeing among branches that milktransparency, I am compelled to look inside, for fear that there will be some unwanted, nestling there, that I must rescue. Some shivering thing delivered onto the grotto steps. That's how many stories we heard. How many bleak court rulings seeped in early, via routes oblique. The details blur and I cannot tell you what exactly happened when these women—mere slips of girls—*could not*. But I do keep peering, sidelong, into bags. When foxes cry, childlike, I cower, still, away from the prospect of sudden adoptive, adaptive, enforced maternity.

*

In 1922 and also, somehow, now, this '[t]he very idea of Birth Control resurrected the spirit of the witch-hunters of Salem,'[vii] and so even with all those media-policing rules in place, 'the women would find themselves thrown about like so many footballs.'[viii] A spokesperson on the radio is saying over and over again, 'babies babies babies do you mean to say that you support the killing of babies' and another is just spitting bitumen and the source of all this rage and panic really is, I think, a 'deep feeling over a matter of property.'[ix] We: The Field.

Meanwhile, the campaign advances, in fits and flurries. Facebook feeds photos of raucous marches. And I have to remind myself that there's a whole lot of much less condign feeling swilling about out there. Over there.

And 'Still the liquid trickled irresistibly down'[x] she says. Back in the air above my breakfast table, the debate, now, has moved on to acknowledge an appallingly secret industry in abortion pills. 'A secret well kept'[xi]/ 'set you right in a jiffy'[xii]   more or less

albeit alone, against the law and with no option to seek treatment if anything (else) should go wrong.

*

In my kitchen, a politician, a repealer, is describing how every day in that tiny place, three other women, less mobile, less insulated, than she, we, lie down on the floor, on a towel, to wait.

And even as everyone unexpectedly has to acknowledge that these little winged pill-parcels are zooming out along the distribution lines of An Post, in the self-same moment they are having to admit that, yes, these teenagers without any other means of action, without the money to travel—are making, in Sanger's ever-stained terms, 'desperate appeals to aid them to extricate themselves from the trap of compulsive maternity'—[xiii] they are also, officially and actually, breaking a most extremely unnatural law. For while 'Limits surely there are to the subservience even of those who must sternly execute the law,'[xiv] and *surely* no chubby Garda is rounding his shoulder to stove in any bathroom doors right now, 'risking 14 years' (in prison) as the woman from the Abortion Rights Campaign is now acknowledging is 'not an ideal situation.'[xv]

*

Rewrite the following sentences in the past continuous:

    To have told no one

    To have them that knew what happened forget, judiciously.

    To have left school early that day

    To have bled out behind a statue of the virgin

    To have held what was withheld within her very name and yet to have failed to find it in time when 'still alive but haemorrhaging heavily'.[xvi]

    Love. Ann Lovett.

Her unmaking owing not to 'some real or misdiagnosed weakness of health'[xvii] but only, indeed, to th'atmosphere asphyxiate. That, and 'an age-long conspiracy of prudishness.'[xviii]

    To bequeathe such an image as would 'would make every self-respecting woman want to fight'[xix]

*

    Small. Thinner, at 9, than she should have been. Wearing the hugest possible coat. Satinish lining / underclad ribs. Collar twitches nose. The child, just today, is in a Real City—citizen of The Crowd. When suddenly, right in her face: a pictured mass, a mess actual, unavowable. Wet redness, screaming type. This pamphlet somehow is already in her, in my hand. Invasion of her very body.

But then my mother (the kindest, softest, warmest) is a woman made remade: whirling, clawed, fierce of voice. The mother is almost unfamiliar in this new posture and so loved, squaring the girl away from this undigestible, this gross incursion on her childhood, on the prospect of her eventual bodily sovereignty. Space hiccups; the woman-hater who thrust that un-thing between my fingers is swirled into the vortex of my mother's fury.

Then she began to feel a special interest in woman suffrage.[xx]

~ Sarah Hayden

The above is adapted from a text written for the 'Women Writing Suffrage' event which took place on Bedford Square on March 17th (the national day) 2018.

[i] 'the difficulty medical professionals have in defining where a threat to health becomes a threat to life'- *Report of the Joint Committee on the Eighth Amendment of the Constitution* (December 2017), p. 8.

[ii] 'particularly relating to the timing of critical clinical decision-making in saving a woman's life'- *Report of the Joint Committee on the Eighth Amendment of the Constitution*, p.5.

[iii] 'over-emphasis on the need not to intervene until the foetal heartbeat stopped'- *Report of the Joint Committee on the Eighth Amendment of the Constitution*, p.35.

[iv] 'The second complaint in relation to the abortion issue concerned the use of the word "abortion"'- Tim O'Brien, 'Broadcasting body rejects complaints about RTÉ's coverage of abortion', *Irish Times* (June 29, 2017) www.irishtimes.com/news/ireland/irish-news/broadcasting-body-rejects-complaints-about-rté-s-coverage-of-abortion-1.3138015.

[v] 'But the angel assured her, "Mary, you have nothing to fear. God has a surprise for you'- Luke 1 29-33.

[vi] 'down through the social oubliette'- Loy, 'The Child and the Parent, Chapter VII, "Ladies in an Aviary"': YCAL MSS 6: 1/1/15.

[vii] 'The very idea of Birth Control resurrected the spirit of the witch-hunters of Salem'- Margaret Sanger, *Pivot of Civilization* (Washington D.C.: Scott-Townsend, 1922), p.14.

[viii] 'the women would find themselves thrown about like so many footballs'- West, 'A Reed of Steel: Essay on Mrs Pankhurst from *The Post-Victorians*', p.254.

[ix] 'deep feeling over a matter of property'- West, 'A Reed of Steel', p.247.

[x] 'Still the liquid trickled irresistibly down'- Djuna Barnes, 'How it feels to be forcibly fed', *New York World Magazine* (September 6, 1914), p.5. digital.lib.umd.edu/image?pid=umd:91977

[xi] 'A secret well kept', Loy, 'Virgins Plus Curtains Minus Dots' (1914), in *The Lost Lunar Baedeker* (New York: Farrar, Straus & Giroux, 1996), ed. Roger Conover, p.22.

[xii] 'when we get back to town, you'll just please run along and see a doctor. Sir Digby Bing, the big woman specialist- - set you right in a jiffy'- Loy, 'The Child and the Parent. Chapter IX: "The Dissatisfied Bride"' YCAL MSS 6 : 1/1/17.

[xiii] 'desperate appeals to aid them to extricate themselves from the trap of compulsive maternity'- Sanger, *Pivot of Civilization*, p.30.

[xiv] 'Limits surely there are to the subservience even of those who must sternly execute the law'- Barnes, 'How it feels to be forcibly fed'.

[xv] 'risking 14 years (in prison) [...] not an ideal situation' – Rebecca Lumley, 'Three Irish women a day order abortion pills online, as study finds them 'safe and effective' (May 17, 2017) www.independent.ie/irish-news/news/three-irish-women-a-day-order-abortion-pills-online-as-study-finds-them-safe-and-effective-35727076.html.

[xvi] 'still alive but haemorrhaging heavily'- en.wikipedia.org/wiki/Ann_Lovett.

[xvii] 'some real or misdiagnosed weakness of health'- West, 'A Reed of Steel', p.245.

[xviii] 'an age-long conspiracy of prudishness'- West, 'A Reed of Steel', p.261.

[xix] 'would make every self-respecting woman want to fight it'- West, 'A Reed of Steel', p.255.

[xx] 'Then she began to feel a special interest in woman suffrage'- Rebecca West, 'A Reed of Steel', p.251

Mná: Is Gnáthóg Sibh

Rann

a single domestic house fly
of undetermined sex
a woman

she was the size of the head of a beautiful man
she was health and health's irrelevancy
she was already herself, entering the bottle
drinking the wine, drinking the wine
she had gone on holiday with the problems of language –
a scarlet worm
they had lost interest in the lecture
the worm had drowned
differently cursed, also
she had realised the record of her movements
and exaggerated them, anticipating the graph form
the plotted erratic deliverance
journey out of neck, towards mouth, solving
the non problems of being beautiful
and smelling great
and having eye jewels and seeing light
in pure prisms even through the green glass
through even the wine drops less sweet
than every echo of her flight compounded
in consequential remarks to the readers of the report
on her

from this fly derives the law
life's curtailment around her
precise & gluttonous eggs
regard: present lack of esoteric
look at the island whole
a day and a night to
mither over fifty women
own one and fill her up
good: so you're a famous KING
This will take 1000 years,
sit down
you'll have no inkling of my sex
nine months will pass like a single day
foster some inherited displacement
say:
I had a son more than once

It will take a day in all, so
to make home
flood with wine from the upturned bottle

an interlude: on the essence of the brand pest spray RAID
containing a natural ingredient aka excessive balance aka fumigation
aka they came from the bins aka can the bodies be found aka do
they just dissolve aka no aka fetch the broom aka I'm leaving you do
it aka this won't be spoken of aka they'll come back aka they won't
come back, I'll never sleep here again, I will rest *on* the window aka
they're in the bath & this isn't like Aristotle said it would be also
know as soon as this door opens: I leave, they enter and kicking away
phenomenal restrictions we'll board a boat as I can't fly

we have been visited by a minor plague. I love it

these flies are used to render us
predictive

The Lord said: if you didn't want me at my fly, you don't deserve me
at my human

                              Tan light sweeping reeds
                              I'll cut and dry this American
                              an unpostable weed
                              Montbresian orange to khaki flag
                              stubborn as local rocks

each night I crawl under a table with fists of bunchéd paper and
press a thumb into the long spine of a creature with no bite

help I am looking for a moment of personal détournement
non-Cartesian and stupid vessel landing on my mirror and my face
it's clear from any spot you'd pick on the wall how ungridlike
her path will be

From unto this fly is a law unto itself incredulous, conceivable
I have to spell this out
I am not Étain
Étain is daily on the sea
and I am at work here
[...]
There's not a question of keeping or not keeping
There's only carrying and walking away: someone tells
Étain

in my basket now an essay on the cruelty of mothers and a battery-
powered tennis racket that will kill her
instinctively retreating to the grotto, to love it, an other emerging of
self and the long gone boy
if I am to claim a home I will have to find her
and here is the problem, the reverse of 'they' as pronoun, singular:
who IS sí

labhair sí
is bean mhaith í
buaileadh í
seo chugainn í
tá mé chomh hard léi
is eol di é sin
tá ocras uirthi
ní racadh sí
an bean óg í? SEA
duine ar bith ach use
racaidh sise ann agus fanfaidh seisann anseo
ise a dúirt é

her is so many
her is every woman I see terminal
her is just one who had no hand in me
who unhanded and returned
and so to point a finger is alike
to biting thumbs to wave and then
salute the nation of non-birth
bending the reeds into the shape
of crossness, exile, bile, milk
a suckling republic gums its coast
Mná: is gnáthóg sibh.

~ Caitlín Doherty

Radical Doula *

'As soon as midwifery changes to gynecology, women are removed from the conversation as healers.'
Deirdre Cooper Owens, PhD.

Doula: (n.) a woman who gives assistance and advice to a new or expectant mother, either informally or professionally; esp. a woman (typically without formal obstetric training) employed to provide guidance and continuous support during labour.
Oxford English Dictionary

N. ^Doula. *A person trained to give free, compassionate care and physical, emotional and informational support across the spectrum of pregnancy.* The Doula Project of New York City

supporting each other
                drawing water
                                out of
                                        the well

            narratives pieced together
                                from fragments and inferences

            medicinal racism

        bear/s his name
                    Dr. James Marion Sims – operating on enslaved
Black women and
Irish immigrants   access to   enslaved people's
bodies
                                        forced
            availability of Black women   's bodies

Doula: from modern Greek 'servant-woman'; from Ancient Greek 'female slave'

[American] origins of gynecology
                                  built on
              the *broken* bodies [of]
                                            enslaved
                              women
                                  Anarcha Betsey Lucy
Mary Smith – a poor Irish immigrant woman in New York – did
not anaesthetise her – made her work "loathsome creature"
filtered through the /patronizing and offensive/ voices and
perspectives of white men they were all   white   men
              centre these women's stories: 'they helped him birth
                                      a new field'
                  we can   read   between
              the lines
                              we can   disrupt
              the silence

just want to be heard
                  listen and don't assume
                                  squeeze her hand

Full-Spectrum Doula: A person who brings the doula model of care to any
pregnancy discourse and outcome, including miscarriage, planned abortion
or medical termination, stillbirth, surrogacy or adoption.
Offbeatdoula.com

assist folks receiving
                  abortion care
urgent need   for doulas
                          Ireland, 2018
          abortion doula
                  bringing abortion into being

                  i go with her
                                  into the procedure room
helping her settle

                    discomfort
        twisted politics   high levels of
        stigma
        ·   distinctly [gendered] suffering

i am a white. cis. woman. who. has been. pregnant. //   and
who. has had. an abortion.   nobody. can take. that
experience. away   from. my body

just want to be heard
                    listen and don't assume
                                              that is the essence of

        doula work

                    this work is   transformative

        history of women
                              supporting
                                          one
                                          another

listening and
        hand-holding
                                              just want
                                                      to be

        heard
        a smiling face
                    at the bedside
                              continuous uninterrupted
                                                      support
                                                              :
                                                      squeeze her

                                                      hand
                                                      providing
                                                      reassurance

you are brave
you are worthy
you are strong

i am sweating
awake
on the table
during
an abortion
the pain is intense
procedure
is
cramping
is
very
doable
but
is
pulling a red root from the knotted flesh of my womb
~~sometimes~~
painful
and i dive into breathing / / /

breathe through
and i dive
uncomfortable
moments
into breathing

my belly is hot [and] the heat makes me sweat

knees up and open / speculum

nurse with gold horse necklace / holds my hand / i ask /about
the necklace ~ she says her daughter rides
then hides   it away //
my legs in the stirrups   :   shaking / / trembling
with tension   :
holding all that pain

112

                              that grief
                                   [that love]

                                        endeavouring to offer
                                                   your heart
                                                    to others
                                                   whichever
                                                      choices
                                                          they
                                                        make

suction pipe – into the speculum – into my cervix – into my
womb   hand-pumped.   hand-wrenched.

              would not   uproot /// – hanging on for life [in the
earth of my body].   dark in there
              and warm >

                         good for a seed / to grow /

                                             'some brief
                                                suction'
                                   seems never ending
                                              'a quick
                                              examination
                                              of the contents
                                              by the doctors'
every time they remove the vacuum   and look   at
each other   ~   my three wise doulas   ~   and
shake their heads and it continues

                            three times
                                             'and the
                                             procedure is
              then it is done
                                             over'
                                             under
                                             ten minutes
                                             including

                                                    set up
                                                    and
                                                    clean up

                        i offer
                        blankets
and my body begins to shake
            with the cold
                                                    of shock

[my] legs shiver and [my] lips chatter silence
                        put cool cloths
                                on her
                                forehead
                                hot pack
                                to place
                                on her
                                abdomen

i am bleeding lightly
                                there is not too much pain /
[and the sickness has
                                probably gone]

    i sit up and stare out the window. autumn leaves. deep magenta
        on a tall maple against the clear blue sky. ruffled by wind.
                                        breathe through
                                        uncomfortable
                                                moments
breathing in purple maple leaves blowing

        breathe out clear blue sky

                        breathe in
                purple maple leaves

                        breathe out
                        blue sky

                            114

breathe in
purple maple

breathe out
blue

stroke her
forehead
explain what's
happening
continuous
uninterrupted
support

'mostly
I'm a
handholder
a breathing coach
a smiling face'
as old as
childbirth
itself

* <u>Note</u>

This text is inspired by Miriam Zoila Pérez, known as The Radical Doula, whose work as a doula includes social activism for Reproductive Justice around intersectional issues of gender, race, sexuality and class. Pérez's practice encompasses the work of a 'full-spectrum doula' – a doula who will assist a person throughout the full spectrum of pregnancy issues and outcomes, including voluntary or necessary abortion. This poem writes through some of Pérez's writings on the subject of her work and includes additional research by Deirdre Cooper Owens, PhD into the medical history of gynaecology in America. The Doula Project of New York City and the DIY Doula Zine, as well as Offbeatdoula.com, are also valuable sources of information and tips for self-care around abortion experiences. Textual sources include:

radicaldoula.com
radicaldoula.com/2011/01/06/my-first-day-as-an-abortion-doula/
rewire.news/article/2018/06/01/women-behind-statue/
rewire.news/article/2017/08/24/statue-rethinking-j-marion-sims-legacy/
www.doulaproject.net
www.diydoula.org
offbeatdoula.com/fullspectrumdoulas/

Interwoven with this research is my own experience of having a conscious surgical abortion procedure in September 2015. This text is written with the intention of performing a ritual/role/service as a 'long-distance doula'[1] for the birthing of conscious and supported abortion practices in Ireland following the vote to Repeal the 8th Amendment in 2018.

This text is dedicated to Mama, Marnie, Sarah, Joe, and all people choosing and supporting abortion for any reason.

~ Sally-Shakti Willow

---

[1] diydoula.org

Uprising

'Can you help?'

The words small, the request
so great. Swelling with 35 years
of stifled rights, the weight of a
million women, hushed and pushed
and rushed across the Sea
to be 'Somewhere Else's Problem.'

'Can you help?' typed quickly, hopeful
sent in anticipation of a change
decades overdue.

The responses come like a burst dam.
A trickle, a flood, a surge
of sisters who can
no longer be silenced.

'Yes, I can help.' 'What do you need?'
'I'll fund your flight.'
'I'll drive you there.'

I'll wait with you, and hold your hand
and promise you, as we stand
together, that we'll never
have to ask again:
'Can you help?'

~ Kate Went

RU 486

'that they may take no hurt neither from Offspring that was that wicked
devil by virtue of this same shield which was named Killchild.'
—James Joyce, 'Oxen of the Sun,' *Ulysses*

it is an obstacle
obstruction   prevention (9/10th of the law)
this occupation   colonial
occupational   (health)
            (hazard)
where what persists is legal fiction
his shield/shielding him
his same shield which was named KillSavitaHalappanavar

it is (offered) for milly but not for molly an
umbrella   a sunlit wall
shelter dependent on w/him

it is (still) (not) available
150, 000 women on waves   in exile
    bitter pill   she swallows
legal or not   she swallows
to author her own contract/ions
contragestive yes she said I will Yes
hail molly, repeal the 8th

~ So Mayer

From *Transpositions*

The following two pages are from *Transpositions* (2018), a collaborative artist book written by Sophie Seita and designed by Jasmine Brady. *Transpositions* is also a prop in a performance of the same title, presented at the New Hall Art Collection, Murray Edwards College, Cambridge, on 24 October 2018. When unfolded, the back cover of the book is one tile in what we call a portable cornfield.

TRANSPOSITION:
White

How would you like to be reproduced? How often and where?

How many pulses do you have to give, do you give yourself, how many do you need?

When and in which contexts have you remade yourself, your tongue, your life?

'What is the relationship in your life between maintenance and freedom?' (Mierle Laderman Ukeles)

We only have a corn field of commonplaces.

A thick white slab.

That touches everything.

X: everyday walk in grass

Y: hold

X: everyday bend knees

Y: everyday bend something

X: everyday sit

Y: shift

X: everyday make a sound

Y: fulfil yourself apparently

X: everyday a little return

Y: sweep clean

X: follow?

Y: repeat

X: in the future there will be the abolition of the chemical in its unquantifiable position it will be demolished and it will clear tracks it will make way uncontaminated it will press on with surrounding sound against the encircling so the recalcitrant spirit will never atrophy in the setting the instituted form the undoing of the pure

Y: at the fence there is some longer grass it is sharp and it buds

How would you like to be reproduced? How often and where?

How would you like to be reproduced? How often and where?

TRANSPOSITION:
Gold

The sienna of its shell dulls the glimmer of the sand.

It glazes as if fresh from a swim, as if

freshly returned from the lapidary.

Casting gorgeous mirrors to those who look at it.

Irraditations of a shield that is not armour, nor safeguard.

Maybe the decorative becomes the truly revolutionary emblem.

Unctuous the dew on that magnificent jewel, its rutilant lines,

unaligned, but horizontally interlinked.

All value is imagined. The imagination is our only value.

In full panoply we reach and hold.

•

The body is a yellow index.
All kernels are light switches.
Nimble dancers, sloppy chromosomes,
oh genetic bundles.
She could trace them.

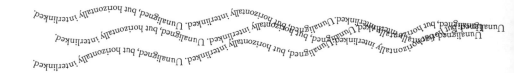

Fade

'The way things fade is wilderness'
Tessa Berring

Peat contains humic acid, a natural surfactant,
which, when agitated by the rapids of a river, foams.

My skin is allergic to Fairy Liquid, so gentle for hands,
and I used to worry it made me look lazy.

Even if you cycle and use only paper bags,
the internet's servers will still breathe out.

Full of asbestos, for fire resistance, the front door
opens and closes, like a poisoner's eye.

In other people's houses, other people's sponges,
towels and grout, give strange little shudders.

Other women are telling me they have fallen
in love with their bodies. I cannot speak to mine.

Something is being farmed, and fed a number
of unspeakable remedies for its ills.

When I am poisoned, I want to rot, unembalmed,
until one day I form foam on dark rivers.

People will wonder about surfactants,
not about whether I am in touch with myself.

~ Alice Tarbuck

ariel

'Why don't you like to be touched?' he asks,
and her voice says *pain*
and her heart says *pain*
and by the time it reaches
the stomach and the vital organs
every window in the house has gone
so the wind can join in
pain
as it blows round the rooms

pain tastes like the sudden iron between
jaws and legs, and this is not a rape poem
she tells him, as she stops him,
this poem can't be a rape poem I will not
let the poem of my life be a rape poem
and he looks at her with as much help
as a mirror, and her fists fly
only to catch on his glass edges, his
glissando as he asks if she'd like an
ibuprofen. 'Where is it', he asks her,
'this pain?' And there aren't any words
about *pain* that aren't void, that aren't
disaster preparedness and the unkept
dark corridor of thinking things.
He says, 'there are breathing exercises,
we could try?' And she thinks, mouth-to-mouth,
let me suck out your air.
And they try, but he isn't
a vessel

his lungs aren't
permeable membranes. He cannot feel it,
he says. He is trying, but he cannot feel it.
And you empty your pockets and pour out
your shoes and there are blades instead of shins
for walking on land:
you go in silence, and every step shouts for you:
pain, pain, pain.

~ Alice Tarbuck

We That Give It

Choice

You'll rip another word from my mouth and tell me it's not mine.
Tell me I want it
Or tell me I don't.

Tell me it's sinful
A yes or a no.

You'll rip the pride from my heart
The dignity from my depths,
Tell me I'm ripping your love from my womb.

But when did I say yes?

Choice:
Yes or No
Words removed from parchment page
Or were they absent from the beginning?

Give them back for my body to hold.

Because even if you don't
I hold them still and won't let go.
No matter whether I hold the babe in my arms,
I'll hold that word and hold onto hope
That hospital wards and white masked bodies
Will not be my end.

~ Caoimhe Kenny

Rebel Girl Repeal

My mama didn't raise a silent girl
She raised a rioter, a rebel.
Not a sit in the corner, plastered on smile girl
She raised a shouter, righteous anger.
My mama didn't raise a good girl
Do what you're told girl.
She raised a no justice no peace girl, a break down the walls girl.
My mama didn't raise a complicit girl
She raised a know what's right, do what's right girl.
Use your voice girl. Fight the man girl. Stand up for them girl.
Fierce as fuck girl
Set the world on fire with your tongue, girl
Feed the hungry babies from your breast girl
Raise the boys with softer hearts girl
Smash the patriarchy with your fists girl

Rise up and Repeal girl.

~ Erin Darcy

The Work and Its Record

Can't separate the work of cutting and gluing the newspaper clippings and organising the meetings and chairing and note taking and making the tea and cataloguing and nursing and protesting and caring and nurturing and washing the cups and booking the buses and decentralising and dismantling power and educating and making the badges and tying the string and folding the box and sending the letters and filing the files and fixing the index and drawing the pamphlets and drawing the logos and listing the agendas and doing the administrative tasks and holding the door open and
writing the songs and singing the songs and singing the words bring back my body bring back my
body bring back my body
to me to the tune of
My Bonnie Lies Over the Ocean
and photocopying the songs and saving them and standing in the picket line at Armagh Jail and refusing to strip and refusing to wash and sweeping the floors and linking arms and booking rooms and booking halls and booking meals from the antifascist work from the trade union work from the work of solidarity from the work of working making money to eat from stopping the BNP campaigning outside trains stations from blocking Enoch Powell's Unborn Child Protection Bill from licking the stamps and posting the letters and lobbying MPs from making love notes on the back of the envelop from signing on from wishing you well and saying Merry Christmas

and writing please call me I cannot pay the telephone from
supporting the miners' strike from supporting the steelworkers'
struggle from blocking Alton's Bill and blocking the Embryo Bill
and blocking Corrie's Bill and the Infant Life Preservation Bill and
the Lord Bishop of Birmingham's Embryo Protection Bill from
writing the newsletter that says dear Sisters from booking the May
Day stall from singing Schoolgirls and Secretaries
Schoolgirls and secretaries working women and wives
Schoolgirls and Secretaries
Schoolgirls and secretaries working women and wives
from leaving a note that says look at page 14 it's horrendous
and reclaiming
the measure of 'survival' from the work of survival
and resisting someone else saying when it is the time of possible
survival and what is the time of possible survival and whose survival is
possible and perceived and
what week of a body of its own weeks does survival start at
from fighting the details of 14 weeks 18 weeks 20 weeks 24 weeks 28
weeks 28 weeks 28 weeks back to 24 weeks from knowing
to survive means what lives next is different
and contains the fight
what survives will not be apart from
what was conceived as she conceived it
what was lived is in what is conceived as survival
what survives is what is prolonged-continued-remade from what was
lived
after and before

      life beyond life
       is not
     made from outside it

the making point of survival can only be attributed to + by she
who has lived

what survives? the work and the tradition of living in the worker
in the records of their songs
the determination is produced from the work done + sung and
cannot be separated from the work of the fight from the work of
asking in the given and perceived moment
who has the right to life?
or from the work of hearing
one song sung to the tune of another's older song

Who's got the right to life?
Money buys it
Who's got the right to life?
War denies it
Who's got the right to life?
Those that live it
Who's got the right to life?
We that give it *

* From a 1980s National Abortion Campaign protest song sheet found in
archives held at Glasgow Women's Library

~ Holly Pester

8

The infinite pain of losing a child
Sometimes only known as a blooming possibility
Expanding like a bubble
The surface swirling in rainbow reams
Stretching and twisting like paint dragged by a brush
The world swirls there too
Reflected in technicolour sheen
Trees, clouds, the promise of an open sky
Pop
Lost in a red hot deluge
Screams and then a sickening silence
And a small chest that never heaves for breath

The agony of a barren womb
Where no fruit can swell to ripe rotundity
Mother dreams murdered
A nursery as bare as the flesh field
A funeral vault for imaginings that haunt
Dusty, greying like linen battered through endless cycles
Each time a little less whole

The crucifixion of endless parades
Playing at perfection
Clawing your way bit by bit up a list
Where ticks in boxes have replaced the stork with its
        newborn scented bundle

Now we bear witness to the disembowelling of fair Eire
Drawn and quartered
Words spilling out
R words
Rights, responsibilities, repeal
And words that are bullets burrowing in meat
Catastrophe, infanticide, murder, rape
And the ugly thing at the epicentre of it all
Abortion
Abortion, abortion, abortion
Abortion of potential
Abortion of a warhead
Abortion of a baby
A baby
A miracle of life
Sperm and ova become zygote become foetus
A foetus with fingers, feet, toes
And soon a heartbeat
The clippety-cloppety that thundered from an ultrasound
The first time my mother heard her child
Like a horse and carriage she said
Mouth curving in loving recollection
And when that foetus is dragged out
A child ceases to exist

Now this is where ethics knots into an impenetrable Medusa mess
Because that child never existed
They were a potential person, a possibility
And the womb that was their home is the inside of a woman
She is not an incubator
Her body is not something that can be hired out without
        her consent
She should not be forced to support a life
Just because she's the one who cannot disown what is sown and
        walk away
Instead there's a stigma and shame where she gets the blame
As if liking sex is a masculine thing
And permitting someone that intimacy should be
        an embarrassment to her and a notch on a belt for him
These are toxic perceptions that serve nobody's need
Outdated mantras that should be ripped up like weeds
Women not vessels
Women with histories and futures and dreams
Plans that come apart at the seams when someone tells us we
        have no right to say
'I don't want my life to flow this way'
Not all of us are born to be mothers
And the situation is gritty for others
Blacked-out nights or lost fights
So don't you dare tell us our rights

That baby's alive
But so are we
Which of us looks more real, it or me?
Which of us do you see?
I'm here
Look at me
Choices shackled but crave liberty
May's the day we have our say
And it's time to repeal the 8th
Repeal, repeal we'll shout to the sky
That baby's real, but so am I

~ Aoife Hynes

The Wave

It made no noise as it swept in,
over field and village carrying
with it the secrets of the deep
and depositing them anew along the shores
of the country from which they'd been spat
and buried deep
under an ocean of shame.

The tsunami poured through cracks and crevices,
carrying whispers and stories that built,
wave after wave, higher and higher,
building to a roar and reaching points thought untouchable,
unreachable, unmouldable, sacred,
holy.

Holy has no place here. We are all sinners.

And with the waves rose the voices of the women,
keening and mourning, shaking loose
the rosaries that held them to their stations,
compliant or banshees, exiled or drowned in a raging sea
but lifted up by the wave, grasped by the others
who heard their cries, reached through waters
and lifted them up for air, unafraid of the voices.

The land is changed.
We have heard the voices from the deep,
the witches they could not drown.
The land is changed.
We have stared and seen the shoes of the desperate
walking from the wave.
Our land is changed.
Is é seo do thír agus tá fáilte libh go léir.
We turn our back no more,
the roar will subside, the waves ebb,
but the echoes will remain.
Ireland is changed.

~ Sinéad O' Rourke

A Chapter Has Closed

Because of You

Because of you,
there is a woman
who walked slowly on old bones
to have her say.

This woman,
who last time
ran the whole way,
holds her head high today.

Her hand,
spotted, shaking,
marks with care,
bears witness to
the cross she carried,
unmarried.

Tears
roll down her face
like she rolled on the bed.
Gored,
the blood that poured
hot
wet
shameful.

Because of you
There is a woman,
who covers her bruises,

who uses 'I'm clumsy'
rather than admit that
he won't listen
when she says no.

She votes and doesn't notice
that she's started to cry.
Silently, hoping,
that the last time
she stood at the gates
waiting,
will have been the last time.

We told you
loving both meant loving neither.
Either you trusted women or you didn't.
You didn't.
You watched while we cried,
and had to lie not to die.
we watched, with love,
while women trusted themselves.

Because of you,
there is a woman
who won't have to sign for
the body of her baby
at the same time as signing for
a parcel for next door.
No more.

Because of you,
There will be women,

who will never know
the flight of shame
bleeding in pain
smiling because
jail would make her other children
orphans.

Because of you.
Because of your bravery.
Because of the lifts,
the gifts of travel.
Because of you,
who despite all the arguments,
who to spite all the insults,
went home to vote.

Because of you,
who they called killer
who they called whore.
Because of you, my loves,

there are women who today are crying
tears of hope and joy and relief
that beneath the veneer of
cheery Gaelic smiles,
the miles their sisters had to travel
were decided to be enough.

Because of you,
women, both relieved and grieving,
will sleep in their own beds.

Because of you,
the damage caused to women,
the dread of the test to women
the dead women
are consigned to the past.

Because of you,
and for which I will never be able to find the adequate words to
Thank You,
women's bodies will be free at last.

~ Dee Dickens

Repealed

I never believed in abortion,
until I started having sex.
And it dawned that,
a mere slip of a condom,
one forgotten pill,
could jeopardise forever
all that I had worked for,
all of my dreams,
but not his.

And in a brutal fashion,
the same rules applied
to survivors of rape,
forced to pay
for another's crime.
To mothers of babies
who will never breathe a first breath,
listening to, 'How far along are you?'
knowing the end has arrived.

Garish lights of Ryanair flights,
will no longer highlight,
our hypocrisy.
The boats will sail on,
but we will travel for business,
for leisure,
not basic healthcare.

Not from a country,
that just doesn't care.

The country has spoken,
young and old alike,
from near and far,
home to vote,
to offer a helping hand.
A chapter has closed,
on crippling shame.
One based on trust,
has finally opened.

～ Sarah Gallagher

Elation

Nervously we waited
With bated breath
A nation hopeful that somehow
We would beat adversity
And do the right thing
Decades in the making
Countless women making lonely journeys
Lying on gurneys in a foreign land
No helping hand from the Irish state
Felt like we were living
In the Stone Age
Verbally tarred and feathered
By the no side
Hiding behind the veil of religion
Or whatever other poor excuse
They used to hurl abuse
At the brave women who did
What they had to do
Every vote counts
And today more than any other
Imagine your sister was forced
To be a young mother
After being attacked
Or told her child would never
Have a full quality of life
The strife one would feel
Is impossible to comprehend
Brave and valiant citizens
Took up arms of knowledge

Of determination and fearlessness
To secure the right to choice
For all future females
Working tirelessly to educate the masses
I tip my hat to you
And on this day my heart
Beats fully in my chest
Today we should be proud
We did it, we did it
We voted yes!

~ Steven Gannon

Relief

In the weeks before D-Day,
our heads held high,
as *Murderer* was spat in our faces;
one word across our chests:
'Repeal'
repeal.
A daring glare,
'Go on, tell me again
that you think you can choose for me?'

Little did we know
that our voice resonated so loud:
the Irish people heard the cries
of women sailing
and flying
fleeing
to the other side of the Irish sea.
They heard our plea,
and on D-Day, they said:
I hear you.
I value you.
I will vote to set you free.

Then,
a sigh of relief ran across the land;
a wind of change shaking the barley
a shiver down our spines

from Dublin to Kerry,
city and country,
young and old:
finally,
finally Ireland rose to her feet.

And yet I just feel numb,
relieved but oh so tired.

Ireland, let me fall asleep
in the cradle of your soft arms,
in the dew of your foggy meadows,
in the night by the fireplace, rain outside;
let me sleep a hundred years now,
comforted that when I wake up
you will be more beautiful than ever.

~ Marianna Donnart

For Whom the Bells Toll Newly

Heard the Angelus ring differently today to me.
For all those who had to cross the sea
whose pain & shame was theirs alone to bear.
Because before today, their nation seemed not to care.

Having nowhere else to go
they packed up all their fears
by water or by air
accompanied by tears.

The votes were made & counted,
the tally in our favor.
How can this nation begin to heal?
It can begin with the repeal.

For whom the bells toll ... newly
A new time for the women of Éireann,
a new shine on the women of Éireann,
for whom the bells toll newly.

Heard the Angelus ring differently today to me.
No more to cross the sea,
no more to take to the sky,
no more to sit in shame,
no more to wonder, 'Why?'

~ Andre Archimbaud

#Repealedthe8th

What a day, the women said, as we passed each other, with our jumpers and badges proudly displayed.

The best day, the women said, as we hugged each other, random strangers and friends alike, in a foreign land, knowing the mutual history that words cannot express.

Did we ever think we'd see the day, us women said, as we pounded our feet into the ground, arms stretched upwards, waking the old Ireland through the disco beat and our ululations of freedom.

Never, we said. Never did we think we'd see it. What a day. What a day for the history books. What a day to be an Irishwoman. What a day.

~ Gráinne Gillis

Acknowledgements and Notes

'Because of You' by Dee Dickens comes from the collection *An Approximation of Womanhood* (2018). 'RU486' by So Mayer was first published in *Molly Bloom* #10. An earlier video version of 'In Our Hands' by Alice Kinsella was published by Choicebox, with the film made by Paul Kinsella. 'Deconstruction' by Frances Presley was originally collected in *The Sex of Art* (North & South 1987, reprinted Shearsman, 2018).

Lightning Source UK Ltd.
Milton Keynes UK
UKHW021118260620
365563UK00011B/783

9 781912 802241